MUSSOLINI IN MYTH AND MEMORY

MUSSOLINI IN MYTH AND MEMORY

THE FIRST TOTALITARIAN DICTATOR

PAUL CORNER

OXFORD
UNIVERSITY PRESS

OXFORD
UNIVERSITY PRESS

Great Clarendon Street, Oxford, OX2 6DP,
United Kingdom

Oxford University Press is a department of the University of Oxford.
It furthers the University's objective of excellence in research, scholarship,
and education by publishing worldwide. Oxford is a registered trade mark of
Oxford University Press in the UK and in certain other countries

© Paul Corner 2022

The moral rights of the author have been asserted

First Edition published in 2022
Impression: 1

Published in the United States of America by Oxford University Press
198 Madison Avenue, New York, NY 10016, United States of America

British Library Cataloguing in Publication Data
Data available

Library of Congress Control Number: 2022932837

ISBN 978–0–19–286664–6

Printed by Integrated Books International, United States of America

Acknowledgements

This book was written during the pandemic—a period in which it was not always easy to confer with colleagues or to access libraries and archives. Nonetheless I owe thanks to many people who helped me in one way or another, despite the circumstances. Not all can be listed here but, for help and encouragement in various forms, I should like to thank in particular, Richard Bosworth, Filippo Focardi, Jie-Hyun Lim, Cecilia Palombelli, Ian Kershaw, and Paul Preston. As always Adrian Lyttelton was a constant source of stimulus even though our occasional lunches in Santa Croce were so dramatically curtailed by events. Obviously none of the above-named has any responsibility for the final product.

The book would not have seen the light of day without the patience and understanding of the editors at OUP—Matthew Cotton and Cathryn Steele—with whom it has been a pleasure to work. I should also like to thank two anonymous readers who made helpful and very constructive comments on an early draft. A final word of thanks must go to my wife, Giovanna Procacci, whose readiness to discuss many of the issues dealt with in this book has been, as always, an invaluable asset.

Florence, February 2022

Contents

Contents

Abbreviations and glossary of terms

confino	domestic exile
fascio	local fascist organization
federale	provincial fascist leader
GDR	German Democratic Republic (East Germany)
gerarca, gerarchi	fascist leaders, local and national
GUF	fascist university groups
INFPS	fascist national welfare organization
MVSN	fascist Militia
ONMI	fascist organization for Maternity and Infants
OVRA	fascist secret police
PNF	National Fascist Party
podestà	fascist mayor of a commune
questura, questore	police station, chief of police
ras	powerful local fascist leaders
squadrismo	violent actions of the *squadristi*
squadristi	violent blackshirt activists, organized in squads
ventennio	synonymous with 'fascist regime' (twenty years)

Soviet ideological slogans get reborn in the mass consciousness, but are mistaken for a reality—a phantom utopia—that never existed

Lev Gudkov
(Levada Center, Moscow)

We remember the past not in order to get it right, but in order to get it wrong

Alon Confino
(UMass Amherst)

We are a country without memory, which is like saying without history. Italy removes its recent past...keeping only those memories, those fragments that might be useful for its contortions, its conversions

Pier Paolo Pasolini
(Scritti corsari)

I

History, memory, and amnesia

Dictators come, dictators go. Very often their departure is accompanied by expressions of popular jubilation, mitigated in some cases only by uncertainty about what may come next. Once a relatively secure stabilization is achieved the verdict is usually undisputed. Three years after Stalin's death, his name could finally be linked to the word 'criminal' in a way unthinkable in the Soviet Union before 1953. With Hitler there was little discussion. When the extent of the Holocaust came clearly into focus (and it took more than a decade for this to happen), Hitler's name became virtually synonymous with evil. More recently, for anyone enjoying Christmas television in 1989, the sight of the bodies of Nicolai and Elena Ceauşescu lying huddled in a desolate courtyard near Bucharest remains indelible. In this last case judgement was immediate. Popular anger directed at the dictator was such that, in defence of the hasty trial and summary execution, the former Romanian defence minister declared that shooting was preferable to the spectacle of the couple being lynched by a mob in the street. And if, for the moment, the North Korean Kim dynasty has avoided popular overthrow, there can be few doubts, judging from what escapees recount, that its eventual demise will not be mourned with copious tears.

Dictators have been accused of most things, often with reason, even if they have sometimes provided useful scapegoats for the difficulties their successors found they had to face. Certain accusations are common. The pursuance of disastrous foreign policies is a charge that can be levelled at many dictators and it is not difficult to think of examples. But it is at the level of domestic politics that they most often seem to resemble each other. Arbitrary power is frequently seen as leading to private enrichment. Whether Ceauşescu's kitchen scales were really made of solid gold remains in question, but the story fits well with what people expected of the man's behaviour, essentially corrupt and self-regarding. Indeed, corruption comes high on the list of accusations made of dictatorships; the deviation of public funds into the private pockets of a privileged elite is judged to be a common phenomenon—a phenomenon particularly galling in what are frequently countries with very limited resources. Any protest against either corruption or peculation is impossible because of a system of justice itself subservient to the political elite and all too ready to interpret the law, even where there is a semblance of legality, in the interests of that elite. Underlying all these problems are the central questions of the denial of rights and the repression of certain liberties—of freedom of speech, freedom of assembly (and of opposition to authority), freedom of movement, and so on. Repression denies people the right to express themselves in a multitude of ways, forcing them to conform to certain patterns set by authority. You are compelled to behave 'as if' you support the regime.

The list of offences is long and would seem to be enough to condemn this type of regime in perpetuity. Yet, surprisingly, this is not so. With the exception of Hitler, dictators and dictatorships seem to be making a comeback in public perceptions. It is most obvious in the case of contemporary Russia, where, according to the Moscow-based Levada Center, there has been a steady rise in the percentage of Russians disposed to view Stalin in a favourable light—75% at the last survey in 2019. In fact, the coffee mugs depicting Stalin and Putin sit happily side by side in St Petersburg souvenir shops. And Russia is not the only example. In Romania, even the once-reviled figure of Ceauşescu has been transformed, with—in 2018—almost 65% of Romanians declaring a positive opinion of their former leader. Although such figures have to be read with due caution, the trend seems clear. In some senses at least, dictators and dictatorships are back in the public eye and that eye is not always unfavourable.[1]

The phenomenon is well known. A further example could be the *Ostalgie* of former East Germans—a reaction to what seemed to many to be the annexation of identity—which attracted considerable attention for a while. Indeed, there is now an academic industry bent on analysing post-communist nostalgia. Very obviously what we are looking at goes beyond the farcical situations of the film *Goodbye Lenin!* or the smoking exhaust pipes of the Trabant tours of former East Berlin—of people essentially just playing with the past. The phenomenon of nostalgia for rulers and for systems responsible for some of the horrors of the past has much deeper explanations—and much more serious implications. In an in-depth interview on the situation in Russia, Lev Gudkov, the prominent Russian sociologist and director of the Levada Centre, suggested that nostalgia for the Soviet era was based on a desire for order, security, social justice, and national dignity. These were factors thought by many (indeed, by the majority) to have been lost in the years following 1991, when the experience of territorial fragmentation of the Union itself and the national humiliation of reliance on American frozen chicken legs inaugurated a period of free-for-all in which only the values of the market commanded any respect. As with East Germans, even a national identity was uncertain for a time. In the case of Romania many of the same factors apply. Ceauşescu, for all his faults, is seen as having offered a stability and a security now absent from a post-communist society heavily dependent on emigration for survival. The disillusion with Western-style 'freedom' is apparent in both cases and the high percentages of people expressing this disillusion suggests that it is shared by more than the old and the poor—the left out and the let down—categories feeling

1. For Russia, see the interview with Lev Gudkov, <www.levada.ru>, 12/05/2021; for Romania there are numerous sites dealing with post-Ceauşescu nostalgia. For one, see <http://you-ng.it; romania-cresce-la-nostalgia>.

they are living in 'secondhand time' and to which these attitudes have been usually ascribed.[2]

It can hardly escape notice that there is a paradox here. Regimes of arbitrary rule, regimes in which you could spend ten years in a prison camp without ever knowing why you were there, are now remembered as regimes that offered order and security. What has happened? Gudkov has few doubts on this score. In the face of present-day difficulties which—and this is an important point—offer little hope for the future, people look back, remove the negative elements from their memory, and construct a new memory based on more positive recollections. In short they create what he terms a 'phantom utopia' of the past, against which the problems of the present can only appear in negative contrast. Here what purports to be memory is in fact playing strange tricks—and the consequences are significant. Regret for the loss of a 'phantom utopia' of an authoritarian past pushes people in the direction of authoritarian solutions to their present problems. In a world that appears to be increasingly chaotic and without order, many look for a 'firm hand' that can restore what is imagined to have been security and stability. As is logical, the reconstructed 'myth' of a socialist society tends towards the rehabilitation of the ruler, now seen as the guarantor of justice and dignity rather than the dictator responsible for coercion and repression.

Russia and Romania are good examples of this renewed authoritarian nostalgia, but the dynamic is not limited to post-communist societies. On a much wider canvas, historically, and despite significant differences with dictators named so far, we might cite Juan Peron's hold on the imagination of the Argentine working class which continued long after his death or the development of the nostalgic Park Chung-Hee 'syndrome' in the Republic of South Korea.[3] Today, in

2. See S. Alexievich, *Secondhand Time. The Last of the Soviets*, New York, Random House, 2016 (orig. Russian 2013); also M. Gessen, *The Future is History. How Totalitarianism Reclaimed Russia*, New York, Riverhead, 2017.

3. See F. Finkelstein, *Transatlantic Fascism. Ideology, Violence, and the Sacred in Argentina and Italy 1919–1945*, Durham, NC, Duke University Press, 2010; Lee Namhee, 'The Theory of mass dictatorship: A re-examination of the Park Chung Hee period', *Review of Korean Studies*, 12, 3 (September 2009).

many countries we can see a weakening of democratic impulses and an increasing desire for a politics with a 'firm hand'. Donald Trump showed scant respect for democratic principles when it came to losing an election but his support remained, nonetheless, very strong among the American public. And while the USA is the most obvious case of democracy in difficulty, many other examples could be cited, particularly in those countries where the right-wing populist movements are growing in strength and where illiberal 'democraships' have taken hold. Present-day difficulties push people towards what seem to be simple solutions; the strong man is one of these solutions. Sometimes it seems that people would even prefer a supposedly efficient tyranny to a corrupt and market-driven democracy.

This book is about Italy and Italians' relationship with Mussolini and his fascist movement. It may seem strange to discuss Italian Fascism and the memory of Italian Fascism in terms of what has been illustrated above and, of course, comparisons go only so far. Every regime is historically specific. Even so, the primary intention of the book is to place the memory of Italian Fascism firmly within the context of what is happening elsewhere in respect of nostalgia for authoritarian regimes. This intention requires an immediate clarification. As a totalitarian regime—indeed the first totalitarian regime—the fascist dictatorship certainly cannot be excluded from the negative characteristics of dictatorships listed above. Yet books on totalitarianism often fail to mention Italian Fascism. Frequently the regime has been relegated too easily to the rubric 'not serious'; films sometimes show a humorous caricature of blackshirt blundering. And, as the leader of a country too often associated by non-Italians with the pizza and the mandolin, Mussolini has been dismissed as a picturesque buffoon, gesticulating ridiculously from his balcony towards a gullible and easily moved audience. Instead, it is important to stress that, as in companion regimes, in fascist Italy there was the same totalitarian attempt to transform people and to transform society. To this end there was violence, hardship, privilege, nepotism, and corruption on a grand scale. And there was a disastrous foreign policy, culminating in the unconditional surrender of September 1943. It is often forgotten (incredibly) that the regime has direct responsibility for some 500,000 Italian dead. Yet, despite this abject record, the attitude of many Italians towards the regime remains ambiguous, and the rapidly growing Italian Right looks increasingly towards the fascist past, sometimes mimicking attitudes and poses drawn from the *ventennio* (the twenty years of the regime). Reflecting his Cold War upbringing, Berlusconi denounced totalitarianism and political violence, but it was always Pol Pot he denounced, not Mussolini.

It is alarming that, almost exactly a hundred years after the March on Rome, people are once again talking about, and warning against, the threat of a new Fascism. Mussolini continues to haunt Italy. If the behaviour of Trump has raised the spectre of a new Fascism at the international level, his Italian *epigoni* have put Fascism back on the possible political agenda. Rehabilitation of Mussolini is thankfully still some way off, but the temptation to look back to the regime as a moment when problems were solved and things got done—in short, when government had the much-admired 'firm hand'—is ever more pervasive. The 'myth' of a 'good-natured', 'benevolent', or 'mild Fascism' (*fascismo bonario, fascismo ad acqua di rosa*) which did 'many good things' seems increasingly acceptable to a collective memory that—always less and less attentive to history—chooses what it wants to remember and forgets the unpalatable rest. Here we seek simply to redress the balance, to present a few facts and figures that can destroy the myth, to respond to many of the current commonplaces that absolve the regime, and to place it where it should rightly be placed— in the company of other totalitarian dictatorships.

It may seem strange to begin a book that is principally about Italian Fascism with references to Romania and Ceaușescu, but the parabola of violent death and a subsequent slow rehabilitation is surprisingly similar. The Romanian leader was spared the mob, as was Mussolini, who was shot, again after a hasty trial, by Italian partisans. But the events following that execution resembled very much a public lynching, even if the fascist dictator was already dead. In Piazzale Loreto in Milan. Mussolini's dead body was hung, head down, from a scaffolding after an angry crowd had kicked it, spat on it, and, according to some reports, urinated on it. The same hatred of Fascism and fascists was reproduced in many village and city squares in the months following the Liberation, when popular fury was vented against those responsible for two decades of repression.[4] At that point, there were, apparently, very few doubts about the 'achievements' of the fascist leader or of his movement.

In those days—April 1945—it might have been assumed that Fascism was finished and that Mussolini's place in history was assured: he was a failed dictator, a man who had brought death and destruction on his nation. But, as with the other dictators we have mentioned, it has not been so. Like Stalin, Ceauşescu (and one might even add Francisco Franco, although he, in a sense, never went away), Mussolini has made a come-back. Some people even speak well of him. This inevitably prompts the question: how is it that a man executed by Italians, reviled by Italians, a man whose body was strung up from the gantry of a petrol pump for public execration by Italians, has become a figure of whom people speak with some regard, even nostalgia? Much the same can be said for Fascism itself. Why is it that the memory of Fascism revolves around what, all things considered, is now seen as an acceptable past, invoked at times almost with a sense of indulgence, rather than provoking a shudder of revulsion? What has happened to our memory of Fascism—our relation with the fascist past—to permit such a turnaround?

Here we are not talking about neo-Fascism, where little explanation is required. The extreme Right needs its heroes and its martyrs to give it some kind of spurious legitimacy and it is only to be expected that the neo-fascist activists still put Mussolini on a pedestal; 'many enemies, much honour' is a slogan that fits perfectly the mentality of an exiguous, if unfortunately growing, minority. What is more

4. See P. Cooke, *The Legacy of the Italian Resistance*, New York, Palgrave Macmillan, 2011. For an up-to-date summary of popular reaction to the fall of Fascism, see also A. Martini, *Dopo Mussolini. I processi ai fascisti e ai collaboratori (1944–53)*, Rome, Viella, 2019, chs 2 and 3.

difficult to explain is the way in which, in contemporary Italian society, in what might be termed a generalized popular memory, the fascist regime has ceased to be seen in totally negative terms. It is not considered to be without its blemishes, of course, and the alliance with Hitler is often referred to as Mussolini's 'one mistake'; yet even here the very concept of 'one mistake' implies that, in other respects, Fascism was not mistaken, that it was acceptable. Strangely, the fascist dictatorship has lost its capacity to shock, its capacity to serve as a reminder of where we don't want to go. Rather, in some quarters, it has come to be seen as a 'good-natured regime', 'a rose-water Fascism', agent of some degree of modernization and certainly not without its original, even colourful, aspects. For some reason Piazzale Loreto has been lost to view. In the same way as we have to investigate the post-communist memory of communism, we have to ask, what has happened to our memory of Fascism?

The most obvious answer is very simple. Our memory has disappeared; we have forgotten. It is now a long time since Piazzale Loreto; the generations who lived through Fascism have largely passed away; direct experience and personal testimony no longer occupy our attention. Moreover our perspectives have changed. Other tyrants, other horrors, have intervened to dim our impressions of the regime and to permit us to cast it in a relatively neutral, at times almost favourable, light. Mussolini was not Hitler is the often repeated refrain; nor was he Stalin, nor (as Berlusconi reminded us) was he Pol Pot—the list is long, and the longer it gets, the less Mussolini stands out from the crowd. Just—and the emphasis is on the 'just'—another dictator, and not all that bad at that. Why make a fuss? After all, as the oft-repeated popular argument goes, in the final analysis Mussolini did a lot of good things.[5]

---

5. For a concise rebuttal of this affirmation, see F. Filippi, *Mussolini ha fatto anche cose buone*, Turin, Bollati Boringhieri, 2018. It is true that the 'anche' ('also') reflects a previous and unstated critical judgement on the fascist leader. The problem is that the 'many good things' has tended to dominate the judgement with the loss of the implicit criticism.

How much truth is there in this judgement? Many good things? It implies that history has been hard on the fascist leader, that the negative judgements generally ascribed by professional historians to one of Europe's foremost dictators have been wide of the mark, perhaps nothing more than the history written by the victors. And popular commonplaces, such as the 'many good things', suggest that Mussolini deserves more credit than he has been given. But does history really bear this out? At this point the ground becomes slippery. In the era of fake news, post-truth, and contempt for expertise, history has a hard time. Sometimes it seems that you can bend it as you like, given that fake news, including fake news about the past, knows no deontological boundaries; verifiable evidence is no longer the determining factor, and facts can be either invented or ignored at leisure. But, in respect of commonplaces about Fascism, we are not talking about history in the strict sense, which, if it is certainly interpretation of the past, has, or should have, when all is said and done, its evidence, its rules and conventions that justify that interpretation. We are talking about what passes for memory, and memory is a more elusive beast. When talking about the past it is essential to keep in mind that history is history and memory is memory; it is essential to distinguish between the two. History tries to explain, it is about causality, while memory purports to record past experience.

Memory concerns the ways in which people construct a sense of the past, the ways in which they seek to give meaning to the past. It does not depend on documents or archives, nor does it necessarily relate to 'facts'. In a sense, memory has no rules, it is a free agent; it might even seem to be each individual looking backwards in time. Yet, paradoxical as it may seem, memory is not just looking back. In many respects memory is as much about the present as it is about the past and if, unlike history, it has no hard and fast rules, it nonetheless obeys certain patterns; for memory is formed not only by what we read about the past, what we are told about the past, but also, more importantly, by what we choose to forget and what we choose to remember, and what we choose to remember is intimately linked to what seems relevant to our present. Memory is the presence of the past in our present.

In fact, societies 'reconstruct' their past, and their memories, according to the prevailing interests of the present, and, very often, according to their hopes for the future. Usually this is not a purely individual process—the apparently straightforward formation of a personal view of the past—but much more a reflection, an 'absorbing', of a 'collective memory' formed socially from current attitudes and discussions relating to the past, from what you see on television and on the internet, read in the newspapers, hear in the bar. Snowball-like, collective memory is a process both of absorption and of addition, a progressing interaction between the individual and the social context. 'Collective memory'—which determines our individual interpretation of the past—is a product of a whole range of inputs of information from many different sources—the so-called 'vehicles of memory'. Where collective memory deals with politics it can, of course, be highly instrumental. We sometimes create the memory that suits us, others may create a memory for us that suits them. Vladimir Putin has skilfully generated a new and favourable memory of Stalinism in order to reinforce his own authoritarianism. What is sure is that 'collective memory' becomes a social view of the past. At this point it is appropriated by the public and generates commonplaces and usually simplified judgements about the past, accepted and often repeated without further reflection.[6]

'Collective memories' may differ, of course, according to inputs, according to interpretation, according to purpose, and according to

6. The literature on memory is enormous and still increasing. On the evolution of Italian memory, see M. Isnenghi (ed.), *I luoghi della memoria. Personaggi e date dell'Italia unita*, Rome-Bari, Laterza, 1997. A useful brief introduction to the changing nature of official commemorations can be found in A. Sierp, *History, Memory, and Trans-European Identity. Unifying Divisions*, London, Routledge, 2014. For a broad summary, see also P. Jedlowski, *Memoria*, Bologna, Clueb, 2000. For an instructive comment on memory studies in general, see A. Confino, 'Collective memory and cultural history. Problems of method', *American Historical Review*, December 1997. For further references to works on the memory of Fascism, see note 11 of this chapter.

which social (or ethnic) group is doing the remembering. For example, in respect of Fascism, the collective memory of the working class is likely to be different from that of the high bourgeoisie, the collective memory of men different from that of women. And, as is widely recognized, a common, shared, vision of the Italian past has been difficult to achieve in a country where history divides rather than unites. There is no single legend relating to Italy's recent past with which all can identify; as a consequence there are different 'collective memories'. What we are concerned with here is one widespread 'collective memory' that has selected certain aspects of the fascist regime and forgotten others. And what has been selected is significant, just as what has been forgotten is revealing. People 'remember' the draining of the Pontine Marshes, the trains running on time (for many, this last has become a kind of metaphor for the entire regime), and some may even point to 'fascist welfare' and the 'social pension' as conquests of the regime. Some may mention new forms of socialization and new expressions of leisure, others point to impressive examples of fascist architecture. Less remembered is the violence, the repression of liberties, the secret police, the colonial massacres, and the constant march towards war of a regime which required above all that people should 'believe, obey, and fight'. A strange amnesia has descended on these latter aspects. With regard to the Duce, there has been a general easing of tension in attitudes towards Mussolini, no longer associated with violence and the destruction of war. His figure has been resurrected as the agent of the 'many good things' and his memory celebrated in all the Mussolini paraphernalia that inhabits so many of our news-stands.

Is this 'resurrection' the product of recent years? Not exactly. In reality the 'normalization' of Fascism, and in particular of the role of the Duce, has a long story and has never been devoid of elements of apology. But if this normalization is in no sense a recent phenomenon, there is—as we will see—a very current aspect to it. To understand this evolution we need to take a closer look at the collective memory that recalls the 'many good things'. Two questions are in order.

The first is straightforward: how far does the affirmation of 'many good things' done by Fascism correspond to the historical reality of the interwar years—as far as we can know it—or is it an idea based on myth and mystification? This verification of reality versus legend is the subject of a large part of this book. The second question has already been anticipated in the lines above. It is more complex and relates to the present day. It asks why so many people today are prepared to share the permissive memory of Fascism and to repeat the mantra of 'many good things' in respect of a violent and repressive dictatorship.

On the face of it, were we to accept the assumption that what people believe today is based entirely on information that can be confirmed or refuted, a credible and well-documented answer to the first question might appear to solve the problem of the second. After all, we can (and will) check the extent (and the quality) of the programme of land reclamation undertaken during the regime (the *bonifica*). Was it one of the 'many good things' or not? But, in reality the two questions, although linked, are less closely connected than it might seem because, as already suggested and as we have seen with post-communist nostalgia, the evaluation of the past is often more a reflection of current problems, disposing us to highlight certain aspects of the past and ignore others, than it is a response to historical analysis. We may even, without fully realizing it, 'invent' a past that gives us some comfort in the present, just as the Russians have invented their 'phantom utopia'. And if, as seems to be the case with fake news, what is decisive is what we choose to believe, what we want to believe, rather than what can be verified, historical fact may be of little use in changing or influencing an invented 'collective memory'. As we have had to learn in recent years, the attempt to discredit political myths with mere facts and statistics is often a frustrating endeavour. All too often, it seems, facts do not matter. There is, after all, overwhelming evidence that Hitler died in his bunker, but there are still many who prefer to believe that, until recently, he was alive and well and living in Argentina.

If this all seems a complicated formulation, with no obvious solution, it is, in large part, because, in respect of Fascism, as with other dictatorial regimes, we are operating on two levels—that of history, and that of memory. These two levels were initially intertwined, but, with the passage of time, they have become separated. What, in the Italian case, were in reality deliberate distortions of history—distortions that often served a precise and sometimes laudable political purpose—have assumed a life of their own, contributing to the formation of a memory that slowly but insistently has moved away from the facts. But to understand how all this started we need to go back to the end of the Second World War.

As is well known, in the negotiations for the peace treaty after 1945, the Italian delegation, in the very understandable attempt to gain the best treatment possible for a defeated Italy, did all it could to emphasize the role of the popular partisan Resistance against the Germans after 1943 and play down the fascist alliance with Hitler. The message conveyed by this strategy was clear: Italians had been on the side of the Allies, it was the fascists who had been the supporters of Nazism. Following this kind of reasoning it was only a short step to the idea that the Italians had been the innocent victims of Fascism, that, in the famous phrase of Winston Churchill, 'one man and one man alone' had been responsible for Italy's behaviour in the Second World War. Fascists thus became the 'Other' and the Italians, as victims—essentially passive victims—of the fascists, were exonerated from any guilt or responsibility. It was a conclusion ratified to a great extent in 1946 with the foundation of the Republic, legitimated by its appeal to the values of anti-Fascism, as though the strong popular current represented by the Resistance had always characterized the Italian people, even during the regime.

Without entering here into the issue of the extent of a popular consensus for the regime (we shall look at this in Chapter 2), it is not difficult to see that this presentation of the relationship between the Italian people and Fascism was, to say the least, rather stretched. It was a line of argument that represented a very obviously instrumental use

of history for political ends and it undoubtedly served its immediate
political purpose. Yet, by positing a distinction between Italians and
fascists—the former innocent victims, the latter guilty perpetrators—
this instrumental interpretation of events created a definite (and comforting) 'history' of the immediate past that underplayed the
significance of the regime and helped to prevent any sustained process
of coming to terms with Italy's fascist past.[7] It was as if the problems
posed by Fascism, the many questions that remained unanswered
about just why the regime had prospered for so long, no longer
required any answer. As the Italian philosopher Benedetto Croce
argued, Italians had been victims of Fascism; they had vindicated Italy
through their resistance to Fascism. Little more needed to be said in
what was now officially an 'anti-fascist' nation. In fact, with the
absence of any Italian trial on the lines of the Nuremberg trial of
Nazis and with the 1946 amnesty that permitted many former fascists
to continue in public life without any slur to their names, the past had
been 'refashioned' and there seemed to be little reason for looking
back. Reconstruction, with all that that implied and promised, concentrated attentions elsewhere, confirming what was, in effect, a kind
of engineered amnesia. International circumstances furthered this
amnesia. With the advent of the Cold War, anti-totalitarianism—
meaning Nazism and communism (the first totalitarian nation was
surprisingly left out)—became the international leitmotif of the West,
replacing anti-Fascism and relegating awkward questions about Italy
and Fascism to the background.[8]

7. The degree to which memory often includes an element of comforting self-justification
is well summed up in the dictum of the Israeli historian Alon Confino: 'We remember
the past not in order to get it right, but in order to get it wrong.'
8. On the role of the Allies in the process of dealing with fascists, see D. W. Ellwood, *Italy
1943–45. The Politics of Liberation*, Leicester, Leicester University Press, 1985. On the leni-
ent treatment of Italian war criminals, M. Battini, *The Missing Italian Nuremberg. Cultural
Amnesia and Postwar Politics*, Basingstoke, Palgrave Macmillan, 2007; F. Focardi,
'Criminali di guerra noi? La mancata "Norimberga italiana" e la rimozione delle
pagine oscure della guerra fascista', in F. Focardi, *Nel cantiere della memoria. Fascismo,
Resistenza, Shoah, Foibe*, Rome, Viella, 2020; H. Woller, *I conti con il fascismo. L'epurazione
in Italia 1943–48*, Bologna, Il Mulino, 1997.

What did this imply for the memory of Fascism in the years following the Second World War? Certainly, in the aftermath of destruction and civil war, there were few disposed to think favourably of the regime and its leader (or, at least, to express such opinions in public). Official memory—reproduced by politicians on formal occasions of com- memoration or celebration—relied heavily on the image of *Italia anti- fascista* and, if personal and private memories of the regime did not exactly correspond to this picture, they remained largely silent and unpublicized.Victimhood suited almost everybody, rightly or wrongly.[9] The net effect of this public emphasis on the later stages of the war and its concluding months of armed resistance was to reduce the attention paid to the regime itself, to the extent that what was pro- duced in popular memory over time was an anti-Fascism without any clear understanding of what the Resistance had been opposing—in other words, we had a militant anti-Fascism without a firmly estab- lished memory of the fascist regime itself. Indeed, the terms of the final stages of the war made it easy to present the Resistance as a war between good Italians and evil Germans, with the responsibilities of the fascist regime, and of Mussolini, pushed firmly into the back- ground. *Nazifascismo*, as the defeated enemy was termed (and still is) was a useful term for muddying the waters. And, with Italians portray- ing themselves as victims of Fascism, this obfuscation of reality was only to be expected; the reasoning was that any responsibility lay with them—the fascists—and not with us—the victims. Thus, in the same way as there was an anti-Fascism without a Fascism, we now had a Fascism without Italians. That fascists and Italians might be one and the same was almost a heresy; it threatened to pose awkward questions and explode the anti-fascist orthodoxy.

The awkward questions, as is now very well known, were asked by the historian Renzo De Felice. In his massive—and much contested— biography of Mussolini, De Felice broke all taboos by asserting that, at

9. See Jie-Hyun Lim's essay on 'Victimhood', in P. Corner and J.-H. Lim (eds), *The Palgrave Handbook of Mass Dictatorship*, Basingstoke, Palgrave Macmillan, 2016.

least in the years between 1929 and 1934, there had been what he termed 'a mass consensus for Fascism'.[10] It was an affirmation that conflicted very evidently with the vision of an Italy 'victim' of Fascism and raised all sorts of issues relating to the extent to which the population at large had supported the regime. More often misunderstood than read, De Felice's biography paved the way for a revision, particularly at journalistic level, of the concept of the anti-fascist nation. What De Felice had presented as a consensus for a relatively brief period was read as mass support for Fascism for the whole of the *ventennio*. His thesis was taken to demonstrate that the orthodox and politically convenient division between Italians and fascists was false, and that Italians and fascists had, in fact, been one and the same. Terms like complicity, collaboration, conformism, and consensus began to appear with remarkable frequency in any discussion of the regime.

There was, of course, a contemporary political dimension to all this. To a large extent the anti-fascist 'myth' had been the preserve of the Left—the good people against the bad regime—and, as always, in the post-war dimension, the political battles of the moment served repeatedly to exacerbate divisions in interpretation. But the implications of De Felice's research could not be avoided. The Italian people were not innocent victims; responsibility could not be ascribed only to not-better-identified 'fascists'. On the face of it, this was a welcome development, a wake-up call to reality. More than one commentator was forced to admit that dictatorships rarely survive for twenty years solely on the basis of repression. It looked like the moment when Italy would have to come to terms with its fascist past, would have to start asking questions about how and why Italy had become and remained fascist, and what this meant for an understanding of the nation.

10. R. De Felice, *Mussolini il Duce. Gli anni del consenso 1929–36*, Turin, Einaudi, 1974, p. 55. De Felice's views were repeated with emphasis in the *Intervista sul fascismo*, edited by M. A. Ledeen, Rome-Bari, Laterza, 1975. A perceptive reaction to De Felice is to be found in G. Santomassimo, 'Il ruolo di Renzo De Felice', *Italia contemporanea*, 212, 1998, pp. 555–63. For a more recent discussion of the debate around the affirmations of De Felice, see T. Baris and A. Gagliardi, 'Le controversie sul fascismo degli anni Settanta e Ottanta', *Studi storici*, 1, 2014, pp. 317–33.

It seemed to presage a time when Italy would have to follow Germany in delving more deeply into its recent past. Instead, by a strange psychological process, Italians remained convinced of their innocence. How? Basically by inverting the negative sign usually placed against Fascism. This was done by recourse to a persistent stereotype relating to the self-image of Italians—that of 'Italiani brava gente' (Italians are good people). According to this stereotype, Italians—by definition intrinsically 'good people'—would have been constitutionally incapable of consenting to an evil regime. Mass consensus for Fascism was read, therefore, as a justification of Fascism; after all, the reasoning went, if Italians are 'good people', and if there was a mass consensus for the regime, then, logically, Fascism could not have been so bad. It was a question of identity. It was as if, in order to think well of ourselves, we had to think, perhaps not well, but certainly not badly of Fascism. Thus a problematic past became no problem and Italians were saved from any opprobrium. If, as victims of Fascism, they had been blameless, now, as supporters of Fascism, they remained equally without blame.[11]

As any historian knows, it is not really a question of innocence or guilt that interests us; these are moral categories that are better left for a different kind of discussion. And repeated condemnation of Fascism without any further explanation or understanding does not get us very far. At the same time, there can be little doubt that these are categories that affect our vision of the past—that is, our memory of

11. See P. Corner, 'Italian Fascism. Whatever happened to dictatorship?', *Journal of Modern History*, 2, 2002. On the 'myth' of the Resistance, see above all F. Focardi, *La guerra della memoria. La Resistenza nel dibattito politico dal 1945 ad oggi*, Rome-Bari, Laterza, 2006. For an excellent summary of the various phases of the memory of Fascism and the Resistance, which also contains a comprehensive bibliography, see F. Focardi, 'Il passato conteso', in F. Focardi and B. Groppo (eds), *L'Europa e le sue memorie. Politiche e culture del ricordo dopo il 1989*, Rome, Viella, 2013. On the European dimension of the 'victim paradigm', see T. Judt, *Postwar. A History of Europe since 1945*, London, Penguin, 2005, and, by the same author, 'The past is another country. Myth and memory in postwar Europe', in I. Deak, J. T. Gross, and T. Judt (eds), *The Politics of Retribution in Europe. World War II and its Aftermath*, Princeton, Princeton University Press, 2000. More recently, on the hazards of a fossilizing memory, see V. Pisanty, *I guardiani della memoria e il ritorno della destra xenofoba*, Milan, Bompiani, 2019.

Fascism. And here we return to our main theme, because, if, on the one hand, we have an official anti-Fascism which, with the passing of time and with its routinization, has become worn and has lost its authority, and on the other we have a Fascism without blame, the path is paved for a vision of the past that has shed its negative connotations. The process of auto-absolution in respect of Fascism inherent in both interpretations (as victims we couldn't do anything else, as fascists we were doing nothing wrong) has led to an approach to the regime that is devoid of responsibility, which, in turn, hinders any deeper examination of what the regime really represented and permits us to forget the negative aspects. The true characteristics of the regime are neglected and ignored—all part of a process that carries us towards what has been called the defascistization of Fascism.[12] It might even be suggested, in passing, that the ever-increasing attention given to the Holocaust in the last thirty years has helped this process, concentrating attention on the evils of Nazism and relegating Fascism, in the public eye, to the role of an innocuous sideshow. In this context Mussolini and his 'many good things' have been able to re-emerge.

That this was happening became evident in the 1990s, with the entry of Gianfranco Fini's allegedly post-fascists into government, with (a little later) Silvio Berlusconi's assertion that 'Mussolini never killed anyone', and with the judgement (since—mercifully—revised by Fini) that the fascist leader was one of the greatest statesmen of the twentieth century. In fact, the more attention was concentrated on the fascist leader, the less people remembered other aspects of the regime, attaching themselves rather to the 'myth' that Fascism had created for itself while still in power. The figure of the Duce served as a kind of decoy from further examination of what the regime had meant for many Italians. Ironically, as memories of the realities of the regime faded with the passing of time and as recent attempts to construct a common, 'pacified', interpretation of the fascist past have foundered,

12. The term is that of E. Gentile, *Fascismo. Storia e interpretazioni*, Rome-Bari, Laterza, 2002, p. vii.

the myth that the regime had cultivated of itself for international consumption—that of a Fascism disciplined, dynamic, organized, and powerful, projected forcefully towards the future—has replaced historical reconstruction, forming a new 'memory' that ignores the enormous gap that existed between the self-representations of the regime, the much-trumpeted fascist 'realizations', and what life had really been like under the dictatorship.

In a sense, it is this 'gap' that is the subject of this book. On the one hand, it is about present-day popular perceptions of the fascist past—the 'stories' we tell ourselves about that past—and, on the other, it is about the realities of fascist domination; it is about what we think we 'remember' and what we have removed from memory. It tries to come to terms with the fact that, in an era of 'fake news' (nothing new, by the way; it used to be called 'false news') we clearly run the risk of constructing a 'fake memory'. We 'remember' what we want to believe, untroubled by fact.

But why do people 'want to believe' in the good works of Fascism? Why is it necessary to write an antidote to what seems now to be a fairly generalized perception that the fascist regime was not really so bad and may, indeed, have much to be said for it? If, as we have suggested, nostalgia is less about imagined past glories than it is about present discontents, and memory is as much about the present as the past, then perhaps we also need to look at the present to understand this slow and steady rehabilitation of Fascism. And here, of course, it is not difficult to find explanations. The instability and uncertainties of the modern world, with globalization, economic crisis, political incompetence, terrorism, the challenge of mass migrations, and—now—pandemics, can easily turn the past into a golden age. As we all know, the past is often rosier than the present; the nostalgia for communism among certain social groups in Russia and other countries of the former Soviet bloc is an object example of this attitude. In the Italian case, the evolution of memory is equally striking. Mussolini represented death and destruction in 1945, but today, with limited confidence in the state at popular level, with a constantly declining respect for the political class, with day-to-day exasperation at the labyrinthine workings of Italian bureaucracy, the Duce is easily transformed (with the help of a few Istituto Luce newsreels on television) into a representation of stability, authority, dynamism, direction—and hope. Not only did he do many good things, but we were respected, we knew where we were going, and we didn't have to lock our doors at night. And so it goes on.

If this vision of the fascist past is very much Mussolini-centred, it is largely because of what we have already noticed—the regime, as such, has taken something of a back seat in the war of interpretations. On the one hand the orthodox post-war narrative has constructed an anti-Fascism without a Fascism, on the other the thrust towards national self-absolution has produced an unquestioning indulgence towards the regime itself. Both positions have left the historical problem posed by the *ventennio fascista*—and twenty years is a long time— as a kind of black hole which requires no explanation. From this void, unsurprisingly, the undoubtedly charismatic figure of Mussolini is able to emerge larger than life. As a result, apart from the few commonplaces concerning trains on time and land reclamation, our memory of Fascism is predominantly political; it is about the dictator, about the assertion and the exercise of power. It revolves around the March on Rome, the speeches in Piazza Venezia, the Concordat with the Church, and the 'triumph' of Munich 1938; it remembers the pose, the gestures, that jutting chin.

Even the advent of cultural history, in its restricted sense, has done little to change the picture. The sometimes highly illuminating studies on fascist art, architecture, literature, and ideology tell us a great deal about the message the regime was trying to communicate, but usually say little about the economic or the social. Consequently the 'political' dominates; almost inevitably with a dictatorship, the perspective tends to be top-down rather than bottom-up.[13] What is missing is a memory

---

13. Before social history fell from grace, excellent studies were produced in the 1980s by the historians around Franco Della Peruta; for example, M. L. Betri, A. De Bernardi,

of how ordinary people lived and worked under the regime, a reconstituted 'social' or 'popular' memory of Fascism. Somehow this has been lost, certainly with the passing of time, certainly because one of the main vectors of the popular anti-fascist memory—the working class—has disintegrated under the impact of neo-liberal individualism, but possibly also because the Italy of the 1930s—predominantly agricultural, poor, badly housed, and, in many areas, badly fed—has become an Italy with which, as a consequence of the economic miracle, it is hard to identify. This makes it more difficult to assess the impact of dictatorship in 1930s Italy; it belongs to a world we no longer inhabit. Yet any 'authentic' memory of Fascism (if such a memory is possible) should have the peasant, the worker, the shop assistant, and the housewife present just as much as the dominant elite and the dictator.[14]

If we are to return to a picture of Mussolini not coloured by a facile acceptance of his self-generated myth it is essential that a more complex memory of the regime be constructed. This question involves putting the 'many good things', such as they may be, in a broader context, one that includes not only new towns and trains on time but also violence, racism, war, and hardship. Just as we do not judge Stalinism exclusively on the basis of the construction of Magnitogorsk or Nazism on the basis of the building of the motorways, we should not judge Italian Fascism on the evidence of single policies and projects, but as a carefully constructed *system* of domination. Yet, to understand this system under which many Italians were undoubtedly victims, we need to go beyond the thesis of the 'anti-fascist nation' and the persistent 'victim' paradigm. We need to contest the simplistic 'fake memory' of Fascism, one that has constructed an image of the regime and, in

I. Granata, and N. Torcellan, *Il Fascismo in Lombardia. Politica, economia, e società*, Milan, Franco Angeli, 1989. Some of this material has found its way into one of the few later attempts at a comprehensive social history of the regime, P. Dogliani, *Il fascismo degli italiani. Una storia sociale*, Turin, UTET 2008, reprint, with updated bibliography, 2014.
14. For a move in this direction, see R. J. B. Bosworth, *Mussolini's Italy. Life under the Dictatorship, 1915–1945*, London, Penguin, 2006.

particular, of its leader adapted to present-day anxieties, one that has removed from memory the less palatable aspects of the dictatorship and forgotten its heavy responsibilities. In some sense Fascism, the 'really existing Fascism' of everyday experience, needs to be 'put back' into the history of Italy—we need to acquire Fascism as part and parcel of the national history—but it should be put back in the correct terms and not on the basis of comforting myths and mistaken commonplaces.

2

'Good-natured Fascism'

Exploding the myth

Sometimes dictators get compliments from surprising quarters. When the former President of the European Parliament, the Italian centrist politician Antonio Tajani, suggested in an interview that 'Mussolini also did many good things', he was subjected to a wave of international criticism, louder, perhaps, outside Italy than within. He defended himself by saying, very broadly, that this was common knowledge and that he—a former militant monarchist—was doing no more than state the obvious. For him, as for many others, a commonplace was common knowledge and common knowledge did no more than reflect the facts. Tajani might have done better to plead simple ignorance and apologize, but the fact that he did not (at least not immediately), that he initially played the part of the unjustly offended, brings many questions to mind, the principal of which must be: Just how did we get here? How is it that a major representative of the European Union can defend the principal ally of Hitler and—perhaps equally revealing—show surprise when such a historical judgement is questioned?[1]

Tajani, of course, is not alone in this favourable judgement on Mussolini. Nonetheless, the Tajani episode provides an excellent example

---

1. For the Tajani incident, see *Repubblica*, 14 March 2019: '"Elogio" a Mussolini, Tajani contestato all'europarlamento: Parole indegne, le ritiri o si dimetta'.

of the fascist 'myth' in action. Here the word myth does not mean fable; rather it relates to that complex of ideas, images, impressions that form a mental picture of a historical event or period. It is composed from a great number of inputs, some consciously acquired, many less so. The fascist 'myth' is just such a complex phenomenon, now very rarely the product of direct personal experience. For some it may be based in part on popular presentations of the regime in the media, including an uncritical viewing of those newsreels shot by the fascist-directed Istituto Luce,[2] seen so often on television; for others it reflects the tendency to take a single aspect of the regime which can be presented in a positive light (in Tajani's case, the programme of land reclamation) and extend that positive reading to the entire regime. Others continue to be mesmerized by the figure of Mussolini, the great leader. Lurking behind these various approaches is the continuing heavy influence of Fascism's own view of itself—the self-representation of a regime that projected a propaganda of triumphalist modernization which impressed not only a large number of Italians but many foreign observers as well.

It is crucial to remember that the fascist regime created its own myth during its twenty-year existence; as with the Soviet Union, the regime was very adept at constructing an image of itself which people were supposed to take as truth and to internalize. Rhetoric often replaced reality. The historical problem is that much of this fascist-generated myth, much of the rhetorical illusion, has survived to the present. There has been a kind of mental disconnect. Looking back, we see the cheering crowds in front of the balcony in Piazza Venezia, not the dead in Ethiopia, Greece, North Africa, Yugoslavia, Germany, Russia, and, of course, Italy. We find it difficult to picture the demise in 1922 of what was, certainly, at that point, only a very limited democracy.

---

2. An institute set up in 1924 with the primary purpose—novel at the time—of producing propaganda films and newsreels.

It is evidently difficult for many to avoid being influenced, at least to some extent, by this myth, which, with the passage of years, seems to become stronger rather than weaker. The reasons are clear. As strong nationalisms appear on the European scene once again, segments of the European political spectrum move closer to those values that Fascism represented; thus it becomes easier for some people to recognize themselves in those original fascist values. After all, the primacy of the nation, one of the principal tenets of fascist ideology, was not so different from the kind of national assertion advocated by our contemporary national supremacists; 'Italians first' is a slogan Mussolini would have had no difficulty in underwriting.[3] What appears nowadays to be a gradual drift—not only in Italy—towards a new authoritarianism may make aspects of the fascist myth seem more appealing than they used to be. Because of this the myth can grow in force. This poses a problem for the historian, which is that, for any realistic assessment of the 'achievements' of the regime, it is first necessary to explode the myth that colours our vision. Our job is to try to understand the myth, to see what lay behind it. This means, very often, changing our 'inputs'—in other words taking a new perspective on the regime, a perspective that is not dominated by Mussolini or by what the regime said it was doing or what it was going to do, but relates instead to how Fascism operated and what it meant for the people and the country.

A regime of violence

Changing our perspectives on Fascism requires that we decide which factors define Fascism and which factors are no more than contingent. The programmes for land reclamation, for example, are not a defining characteristic of Fascism, any more than the VW Beetle,

3. The slogan of the leader of the right-wing Lega party, Matteo Salvini. Mussolini would, of course, have had no difficulty in subscribing to a slogan with Trumpian echoes such as 'Make Italy great again'. His core message was precisely this.

commissioned by Hitler, can be called a defining characteristic of
Nazism (and we hear few people disposed to argue today that Hitler
'did many good things' on the basis of the Beetle). Other regimes—
democratic, authoritarian—have reclaimed marshes and produced
memorable motor cars; it was not necessary to be fascist to do these
things. But, if we search for defining characteristics, we are bound to
discover immediately the first of the great absentees from the fascist
'myth' as it stands today—and this is violence. The regime is no longer
associated immediately with violence; the Duce is not remembered as
a man whose power rested at least in part on the cudgel, the rifle, the
pistol, and the knife.

There are many reasons for this. At popular level, concentration on
the figure of Mussolini has distracted attention from the mechanisms
of a repressive regime, producing Berlusconi's 'Mussolini never killed
anyone' approach to the question, as if individual murders were the
only issue. Furthermore, persistent comparisons (often themselves ill
informed) with Hitler (and the Holocaust), and Stalin (the Gulag and
the Ukrainian Holomodor), have served to let Mussolini off the hook;
the body-count seems to speak for itself. Mussolini was, by common
consent, the lesser evil. But from being the lesser evil the path has
been short to him becoming no evil; as if, compared with the 'absolute evil' of the Holocaust, all other evils pale into insignificance.[4]
Even when there has been some recognition of the role of fascist
blackshirt violence, it is a role all too often considered significant only
in the period prior to the March on Rome (October 1922) and treated
as a phenomenon limited in extent and in time—in a sense, as something almost extraneous to the regime once in power. After all, how is
it possible that a man whom no less a figure than the Pope declared
to be 'sent by Providence' could owe his position to crude violence?

4. R. Ben Ghiat, 'A lesser evil? Italian Fascism in/and the totalitarian equation', in
   H. Dubiel and G. Motzkin (eds), *The Lesser Evil. Moral Approaches to Genocide Practices*,
   New York, Routledge, 2004. It is ironic that, by this kind of reasoning, Mussolini, who
   spent many years trying to avoid being overshadowed by Hitler, should in the end be
   'saved' for posterity by the very dominance of his German partner.

At the academic level, the emphasis given over recent years to the ideological and cultural aspects of the regime and even to the subjective and emotional 'meaning' of Fascism has tended to subordinate to cultural factors the role that violence played in the establishment of the regime and in its operation during the entire period of the *ventennio*. In broader terms, one wonders whether there is not a more general problem in remembering violence: it seems legitimate to ask, have the 75% of Russians who look back on Stalin with favour actually forgotten the Gulag? Certainly, in Italy, violence has fallen from view. All too often, the murders of the priest Don Giovanni Minzoni (Ferrara, 1923), the socialist leader Giacomo Matteotti (Rome, 1924), and the anti-fascist Rosselli brothers (Bagnoles-de-l'Orne, France, 1937) have become just unfortunate and embarrassing blots on an otherwise clean sheet. We forget the more than 3,000 direct victims of the violence of the blackshirts in the early years of the movement.[5]

Yet, in order to change our perspectives on Fascism, in order to explode the myth of the 'good-natured regime', we have to start from here—from violence. Violence was central to Fascism from the beginning to the end. There should be no question about this. Physical violence was one of the principal defining characteristics of the regime and it is impossible to understand many aspects of Fascism without remembering that violence, either explicit or threatened, was always present. Moreover, if we want to understand fascists, we ignore or deny the role of violence at our peril, because it was not just a crucial factor in establishing and maintaining fascist domination but a feature built into Fascism's image of itself. It was part and parcel of the

---

5. For numbers, see F. Fabbri, *Le origini della guerra civile. L'Italia dalla Grande Guerra al Fascismo*, Turin, Utet, 2009. pp. XXIV-XXV. This particular body-count is deceptive. The numbers may seem low when compared with the victims of Nazism, Soviet communism, and those of the regime of Francisco Franco. However, Richard Bosworth estimates that deaths directly imputable to the politics of Mussolini could be around one million. See R. J. B. Bosworth, *Mussolini*, London, Bloomsbury, 2001, ch. 1. For victims of the Gulag, see those (much contested) of A. Applebaum, *Gulag. A History*, London, Penguin, 2003; for Spain, see P. Preston, *The Spanish Holocaust. Inquisition and Extermination in Twentieth-Century Spain*, London, Harper, 2011.

fascist—something of which fascists were immensely proud. As many detailed studies make clear, violence was part of fascist identity; it created a cohesion and unity among the blackshirts similar to that experienced by many of them in the trenches during the First World War.[6]

But, if violence is to be brought back into the picture, it should be brought back in its real terms. It was neither occasional nor defensive, simply the product of isolated and random clashes with political opponents. Rather, it was systematic and aggressive; it was an integral part of fascist activity because it was central to fascist ideology. No self-respecting fascist would ever have denied that violence was anything other than a virtuous agent, 'purifying' the nation from its 'anti-national' enemies and removing the causes of contamination. For the fascist, political assassination—murder of opponents in more straightforward language—was simply the justified removal of divisive influences, subsequently glorified as part of a heroic battle 'for the Nation'. The (relatively few) dead fascists became 'martyrs' in the same cause, their deaths consolidating the myth of sacrifice and their funerals often part of an impressive choreography of public grieving.

In fact, far from downplaying the part played by violence, the fascists themselves made the myth of courageous blackshirt activities (*squadrismo*) one of the key legends of the movement, with many ageing activists (*squadristi*) recalling, in the 1930s, the glorious epics of the first anti-socialist onslaught when violence and impunity before the law went hand in hand. One of the standard tropes of the regime

6. The best general history of the origins of Fascism remains A. Lyttelton, *The Seizure of Power. Fascism in Italy 1919–29*, London, Weidenfeld, 1973 (revised edition, London, Routledge, 2003); also A. Lyttelton, 'Fascismo e violenza. Conflitti sociale e azione politica in Italia del primo dopoguerra', *Storia contemporanea*, 6, 1982. For a more extensive treatment of fascist violence, see M. Ebner, *Ordinary Violence in Mussolini's Italy*, Cambridge, Cambridge University Press, 2011. Relevant texts in Italian are G. Albanese, 'Dire violenza, fare violenza. Espressione, minaccia, occultamento e pratica della violenza durante la Marcia su Roma', *Memoria e ricerca*, 13, 2003; G. Albanese, 'Brutalizzazione e violenza alle origini del fascismo', *Studi storici*, 1, 2014, pp. 3–14. On identity, see C. Baldassini, 'Fascismo e memoria. L'autorappresentazione dello squadrismo', *Contemporanea*, 5, 3, July 2002. Specifically on the role of *squadrismo* throughout the *ventennio*, see M. Millan, *Squadrismo e squadristi nella dittatura fascista*, Rome, Viella, 2014.

became that of the moment when they, the heroic few, had confronted and defeated the bloodthirsty Bolshevik hordes, thus saving the nation from a socialist revolution.

But this—the fascist rescue of Italy from the 'internal enemy' of socialism—is a legend. With the idea, propagated by the fascists, of the 'preventive counter revolution'[7]—that is, the fascist revolution to forestall a socialist revolution—we are entering the realm of fake news. This is because, very simply, there was no socialist 'revolution' to counter. Rather ironically, much of the history that has since been written about this period has lent credibility to the fascist legend. The very terminology relating to the years following the end of the First World War—the *biennio rosso* (the 'red years')—has suggested that, faced by a rising wave of revolutionary socialism, the fascists did no more than *react* to the violence of others. Attention paid (particularly on the Left) to the novelty and the dynamism of post-war socialism— the moment of Antonio Gramsci and of the factory councils—has unintentionally favoured the tendency to interpret the fascist movement as a response to this remarkable wave of organized left-wing protest. By this reading black followed red.

In reality, as several recent studies have emphasized, these years were, in a sense, more black than red, with repression rather than revolution the principal feature of the Italian politics of the time.[8] Detailed analyses of the period have demonstrated clearly the extent to which the conservative Italian Right was organizing, more or less from Caporetto[9] onwards—that is from late 1917—through civic patriotic committees and impromptu nationalist *fasci*[10] in the attempt to control a very

---

7. Title of the book by the anarchist Luigi Fabbri, *La controrivoluzione preventiva. Riflessioni sul fascismo*, Bologna, Cappelli, 1922.
8. Fabbri, *Le origini della guerra civile* ch. 2.
9. The battle in which the Italian army was routed by Austrian and German troops, provoking what turned out to be a historic resistance to further invasion on the part of the Italians.
10. The word 'fascio' means simply a group or, with objects, a bundle. It was in common use to describe small associations of like-minded people well before the arrival on the scene of Mussolini.

rapidly evolving socio-political situation, a consequence of the radicalization provoked by the enormous upheaval of the war.[11] It is in this context of right-wing nationalist mobilization that the first fascist actions in 1919—in Trieste against ethnic Slavs and in Milan against the offices of the socialist newspaper *Avanti!*—have to be located. These actions preceded the great socialist mobilization of the first months of 1920.

While these attacks can be attributed to what were still fringe groups of violent extremists, the more consistent repression was carried out by the Italian state, challenged by social protest and unable to formulate any consistent reformist strategy to meet that protest. The sacrifices of the war had made people realize that they had not only duties in respect of the state—they also had rights. Protest at the extremely difficult economic situation immediately following the end of the war sprang from this new awareness. The extent of state repression of this protest in 1919 and, particularly, in 1920 has only recently been fully documented and serves to put the subsequent fascist violence in context. Remarkably, in the year before the fascist squads began their onslaught on the socialist leagues (that is, prior to autumn 1920) more than 600 workers were killed by the police and *carabinieri* and three times that number wounded.[12] The fascist groups developed on the back of this state repression, with the direct complicity, even at times with the direct instigation, of the police and the military.[13] Furthermore—as is now widely recognized—these squads began to operate in earnest at the moment when, in the autumn of 1920, the Occupation of the Factories was over and the socialist agitations in the rural areas were already in decline. The intense phase of

11. See now Giovanna Procacci, 'Il fronte interno prima e dopo Caporetto. Il fascio di difesa parlamentare', in P. G. Zunino (ed.), *Caporetto 1917. Un passo dalla 'finis Italiae'?*, Bologna, Il Mulino, 2020, pp. 145–87.
12. Fabbri, *Le origini della guerra civile* ch.3.
13. G. Padulo, *L'ingrata progenie. Grande guerra, massoneria, e origini del fascismo (1914–23)*, Siena, Nuova Immagini, 2018.

rick-burning in the countryside and of the struggle for workers' control in the factories had already passed.

Of course, there *was* violence on the part of the socialists, particularly in the rural areas of the Po Valley, but it was of a very different nature from that of the fascists. Again, a look at context is in order. Since the reclamation of vast zones of marshland in the 1880s the agriculture of these areas had depended on the existence of a surplus of labour, permitting the proprietors and large leaseholders to keep wages low because of the intense competition for work. Most landless agricultural labourers (*braccianti*) would be lucky to find work for 120 days a year; they lived in extreme poverty. Before the First World War violence had been endemic to the region, as *braccianti* attempted to organize into unions and employers reacted to strikes with the use of blackleg labour and the recruitment of civilian armed guards.[14] Socialist violence operated within the logic of contractual conflict— in the main, through strikes and the attempts to achieve the control of the labour market in order to push up wages. And while rick-burning and the maiming of animals were extreme measures used to assert a contractual position, they were hardly the same as brutal murders of political opponents. When, in 1919–20, the socialist unions finally achieved control of the labour market and began to force up wages (not without violence and intimidation directed at some recalcitrant workers), the structural basis of the economy of the region (low wages) was threatened. The elections of November 1920, with the arrival of socialist administrations in many communes, provided a further shock. The large landowners reacted to the threat of loss of control, first of the labour market and then of provincial administration, with the financing and material support of the first rural *fasci*. And they chose the moment when the unions of agricultural workers were momentarily on the back foot after more than a year of continuous agitation. But it was at this point that the difference in the use of

14. See A. Roveri, *Dal sindacalismo rivoluzionario al fascismo (1870–1920)*, Florence, La Nuova Italia, 1972.

violence became obvious. Instances of labourers murdering their bosses were extremely rare, the opposite—through the work of the squads—extremely common.[15]

What provoked reaction on the part of the landed proprietors and industrialists was not the threat of an imminent revolution; it was the fear of losing political control as a result of (usually reformist) socialist victories in the administrative elections of November 1920.[16] The violence they instigated and supported was in no sense a novelty. Certainly it was more systematic than in previous years and, very quickly, more widespread, and clearly it bore the imprint of the brutal experience of the trenches. Yet in other respects it expressed a strong line of continuity not only with the previous repressive policies of the state but also with the tendency of proprietors—a tendency already seen on many occasions before the war—to turn to the use of private violence when their control was seriously challenged.

Seen in this light, the fascist thesis that *squadrismo* represented a justified reaction to unjustified socialist violence has to be seen as no more than a discourse through which the fascists themselves sought to give some kind of legitimacy to their actions. The fascist 'preventive counter-revolution', as it was termed by one (actually an anarchist) writer in 1922, is a myth that has endured—but it is a myth. Here the concept of 'mass consensus' for the regime, as generalized by the media, has served to cover the reality of what was, in effect, a very one-sided civil war and has obscured the fundamental role of coercion in the establishment and the subsequent life of the regime.[17]

15. For the conflict in the Po Valley, see P. Corner, *Fascism in Ferrara 1915–1925*, Oxford, Oxford University Press, 1975.

16. For example, landed proprietors in the Po Valley feared—not without reason—that socialist town councils would effect an immediate and massive increase in taxes on land.

17. Indeed the very concept of 'civil war' has been the subject of discussion, precisely because it would seem to imply some kind of parity between the contestants. See G. Ranzato, *Guerre fratricide. Le guerre civili in età contemporanea*, Turin, Bollati Borighieri, 1994.

The realities of this first onslaught of blackshirt violence are well known to historians, but seem somehow to have failed to enter a wider collective memory of the regime. As with so many other less palatable aspects of the regime, the brutal beginnings of the movement have been pushed to one side. While we may find it difficult to think of Nazism without shuddering at the idea of the SS, when we think of Fascism the blackshirts remain in the background, sometimes—in film and literature—assuming an almost folkloric character. If we think about them at all we attribute to them a role limited in time and in importance. It is as if the ferocious violence of Italians against Italians does not bear thinking about; we would rather remember the fertile reclaimed lands and the enthusiastic crowds in Rome, in Piazza Venezia.

A brief reality check does no harm. What actually happened in much of central and northern Italy (and in the South, in Puglia) is that workers' organizations were rendered powerless and the workers deprived of any weapons with which to fight the fascists. In rural areas the socialist leagues, responsible for the organization of agricultural workers, were ruthlessly 'beheaded' through a process of elimination of their leaders, often with the complicity of the forces of order and the judiciary, leaving the *braccianti* at the mercy of a labour market controlled once again by the landed proprietors. In these circumstances the agricultural labourers found themselves having to choose between their political allegiances and starvation; those who continued to express socialist ideas no longer found work. Small wonder, therefore, that we find a rapid expansion in the numbers enrolled in the newly founded fascist syndicates from the spring of 1921 onwards—an expansion hailed, predictably, by the fascists as an indication of workers' conversion from socialism and their spontaneous 'consensus' for Fascism.[18]

In industrial areas violence was less explicit—skilled workers represented a valuable asset for employers and could not be as easily replaced

18. Corner, *Fascism in Ferrara*, ch. 7.

as the landless agricultural labourers—but violence was nonetheless instrumental in conditioning the contractual power of workers' organizations. Industrialists were wary of giving too much influence to the fascists, and tended to resist fascist intrusion within the factory, but the threat of blackshirt violence at the gates of the factory served its purpose of intimidation. As with the *braccianti*, industrial workers who resisted the fascist 'faith' and created problems could find themselves without a job, blacklisted, and effectively unemployable. Indeed, in this respect, a further, surprisingly uncharted, area of dissent is represented by the large number of workers, both agricultural and industrial, who were forced to emigrate in the course of the 1920s, going to France and Switzerland because employment in Italy had been barred to them. Whole families packed their bags and left because the local fascists made their life impossible. Many others moved within Italy for the same reason.[19]

Often the manner of murder was verging on the macabre, demonstrating the total depersonalization of the opponent. After armed clashes, socialist workers and farm labourers would be dragged, already wounded, into the town square and subjected to slow deaths. Historian Mimmo Franzinelli recounts the particularly horrible murder of a farmer, Giuseppe Valenti, guilty of having killed a fascist in self-defence. Valenti had managed to escape to the fields after the first, and fatal, encounter with the fascists but, hunted for days by hundreds of fascists brought in from all surrounding areas, he was eventually captured. First severely beaten with cudgels, which broke both his arms, and then wounded in the face by a gunshot, he was strapped to the bonnet of a car and driven 'like a hunted animal, a trophy' through the streets of the town until his captors reached the fascist headquarters. There, bleeding profusely and already more dead than alive, he was subjected to a ten-minute trial in which he was condemned to death 'first by stabbing, then by shooting'. Again paraded through the town, he was carried to a nearby quarry where he was killed; twenty-five

19. Ebner, *Ordinary Violence*, p. 31.

shell cases were found by his body. The *carabinieri*, repeatedly informed of what was going on, made no attempt to intervene.[20] The law existed, of course; there was simply no intention of enforcing it.

Events like this were innumerable in 1921 and 1922. What is striking in the case of Valenti is the public display of what is, in effect, a ritual murder, designed not simply to intimidate enemies and discourage any further opposition but also—perhaps more importantly—to impress onlookers and give the air of an act of legitimate justice to what was nothing more than an ordinary assassination. It was an expression of one of the defining characteristics of Fascism—the sacralization of violence as a means of resolving disputes.[21]

But why insist on these violent origins of the regime? Were they not simply the teething troubles of a movement that would soon out-grow its violent phase and burgeon into something very different? After all, wasn't Fascism the regime of order and discipline? Well, not exactly. The violence of *squadrismo*, particularly in the bitter struggles of the Po Valley, and the ideology that lay behind that violence, con-stituted an imprinting of the movement that would remain a charac-teristic of Fascism for the entire twenty years of fascist rule. A part of the totalitarian vocation began here. Intolerance of any kind of oppos-ition, the disposition to resolve argument through the use of force, the expectation of impunity before the law—these were attitudes that permeated the regime from beginning to end and would, of course, be reproduced, with renewed brutality, under the short-lived Repubblica di Salò.[22]

It is enough to read the reports of prefects and provincial police chiefs to understand that the sporadic and random violence of fascist militants directed at people who had, in one way or another, shown

20. M. Franzinelli, *Squadristi! Protagonisti e tecniche della violenza fascista 1919–1922*, Milan, Mondadori, 2004, pp. 133–7.
21. Ibid., ch. 4.
22. Repubblica di Salò or Repubblica Sociale Italiana (RSI): Mussolini's puppet republic, formed with German support, after his removal from power in July 1943 and the German occupation of Italy following the armistice of 8 September 1943.

disrespect for the regime, was an aspect of daily life not only during the early 1920s but also during the 1930s.[23] Some examples: in 1937 the old men who forgot to take off their hats as the fascists marched by were beaten up, almost—it would seem from the report—as a matter of routine. People who asked for foreign newspapers at the news-stand might suffer the same fate. A convocation to the local fascist headquarters could end badly; as one *segretario federale* (the local fascist leader) put it, 'We dealt with the matter in our usual fashion' and no one doubted what this meant. A similar convocation ended with the person being interrogated 'falling' to his death from the third floor window.[24] And there was general public concern in September 1939 when, in a major speech, Mussolini invited the fascists 'to clean up the corners' of Italy, taken to be an invitation to the fascist militants to resume their violent activities on a large scale. As the historian of *squadrismo*, Matteo Millan has shown, even if its use was less systematic than it had been in earlier years, the fascist cudgel in no sense disap-peared with the apparent pacification of Italy after 1922.[25] It is important to remember this. A memory of Fascism that puts this often-murderous violence in pride of place, that sees violence as one of the defining and structural characteristics of the regime, would be more accurate than one that recalls the trains running (allegedly) on time.

Mechanisms of social control

But, if direct physical violence was never abandoned during the regime—the fascist bully could always be found on the tram, at the

23. It is informative to see, in Galeazzo Ciano's *Diary*, the entry for 22 September 1939 where Ciano deprecates the violent beating of an innocent man ('a patriot and a fascist') by fascist 'gangsters', 'protected by the fact that they belonged to the Party and by the assurance that they would not be punished'. He commented, correctly, that 'these methods are not of a kind to uproot anti-fascism. They create it.'
24. For these examples, and more, see P. Corner, *The Fascist Party and Popular Opinion in Mussolini's Italy*, Oxford, Oxford University Press, 2012, ch. 6.
25. Millan, *Squadrismo*. ch. 7.

market, in the piazza, and his fascist militia (MVSN) uniform seemed to give legitimacy to his bullying—most people would experience fascist control less directly. After all, if you kept your nose clean, didn't speak ill of the Duce, and avoided attracting attention, the fascist bully would leave you alone. Even so (and as these conditional factors suggest), your life would still be determined in multiple ways by the existence of the regime. At work, at home, during leisure time, the regime was present and it was a presence that conditioned existence and often could not be avoided.

Current memory of Fascism seems to have almost completely removed this aspect of the regime—an aspect that can only be called the conditioning effect determined by intense social control. When we imagine Mussolini we rarely think about the system on which his authority was based. It is as if personal charisma were a sufficient explanation for his hold on the Italians, a sufficient reason for his real-ization of an alleged 'mass consensus' for the regime. Again we can notice the very different treatment accorded to Nazism and Stalinism, where attention is often centred on repressive mechanisms and the key role of the SS and the Gestapo, on the one hand, and the NKVD on the other. Conversely the OVRA[26] has failed to enter public con-sciousness and the activities of the PolPol (Polizia Politica) remain largely unknown. It is all just Mussolini.

So was Fascism really so benign? Was it the 'good-natured regime', the 'benevolent regime' of popular legend? The fact is that the more people study the regime, the more it is seen to have many of the char-acteristics of its much denigrated totalitarian brothers. And this is nowhere more evident than in the area of social control. Physical violence, and the continuing threat of such violence, played its part, as

---

26. The significance of the letters OVRA remains uncertain. Sometimes thought to stand for 'Opera Volontaria di Repressione dell'Antifascismo' (but why 'volontaria'?), it is now generally considered to be an acronym without meaning, relying on its associ-ation with the word 'piovra' (octopus) to suggest extensive reach and all-pervasiveness. See M. Franzinelli, *I tentacoli dell'OVRA. Agenti, collaboratori e vittime della polizia polit-ica fascista*, Turin, Bollati Boringhieri, 1999, pp. 103–4.

we have seen, but much more effective in controlling the population in the long term were the sticks and carrots that we associate with all forms of totalitarian domination. Fundamental in conditioning people's attitudes and behaviour was the regime's control of access to both opportunities and resources. With the extension of the bureaucratic state, the regime rapidly permeated most sectors of both national and local administration and was able to impose its wishes through the operation of these bodies. Decisions were frequently made on the basis of political criteria—allegiance to Fascism being the most prominent—rather than on criteria of merit, competence, or need. And suitability for a job, for a licence, for a work permit, or for a pension would be decided at the discretion of the fascist official.

The regime controlled almost all aspects of 'normal' life, apart from the Church, which was itself a further element of control. For those who required a licence or a permit for any kind of activity—even a marriage certificate—the passage by the fascist authorities was obligatory. In order to find a job, workers needed (after 1933) a *libretto di lavoro*—a kind of work passport—which was issued by the fascist union and could be withdrawn in the event of indiscipline. Withdrawal could mean hunger and destitution for the family. Similarly, as already suggested, the concession of a pension could depend on where you stood with the local (probably fascist) pensions officer. And poorer families and old people often required some form of assistance; requests for a subsidy or for enrolment in the communal list of the poor (which gave the right to assistance) were vetted by fascists, and applicants were likely to be subjected to the humiliation of an inspection of their homes by the fascist *visitatrice*—a woman inspector, much disliked because considered a condescending snooper. Following the fascist takeover of many private institutions, much charitable activity was in the gift of the fascist authorities—and what had been given could be taken away. When, in 1937, the local fascist boss in Padua visited a poor area of the city, he asked an elderly woman what she thought about the food parcels distributed by the *fascio*. An observer noted that 'She had the courage to tell the truth about the quality and the quantity, both inadequate.' The next day she had her welfare book withdrawn.[27]

Particularly in the large towns, local fascist organizations kept tabs on families, registering the political orientation of the parents and their past behaviour; eventual employment of both parents and children could be affected if socialist or anti-fascist inclinations had been recorded.[28] In Turin, for example, Fiat went through the local fascist party organization when it wanted to hire new workers and it is obvious who would be taken and who would be blacklisted.[29] By the same token, the privileges that the fascist hierarchy could accord to its loyal followers inspired many to embrace the regime with enthusiasm; sticks were accompanied by carrots and the rewards of a regime that controlled so much were not to be despised. For instance, as social welfare expanded under the regime, access to benefits made conformism the obvious—even the unavoidable—choice for many, particularly for those with families. The same was true when it came to possibilities for employment. Many careers were facilitated because of known fidelity to the regime. The key fact, though, is that probably just as many were destroyed because of what was considered unacceptable political orientation. Discretionary powers meant that the regime always had the knife by the handle.

It was, above all, this discretionary nature of decision-making that rendered people so vulnerable to what was, in effect, blackmail. Conformism was virtually obligatory if you wanted to avoid the attentions of the authorities and the authorities were in no sense neutral. The message was clear: 'behave as we want you to or face the consequences'. It is as well to remember that the New Legal Text of 1926 on public order permitted prefects to send people to *confino*

---

27. Corner, *Fascist Party*, p. 178.
28. For a detailed examination of locally based fascist control, see the sections by Roberta Vegni and Antonio Iannello in V. Galimi (ed.), *Il fascismo a Grosseto. Figure e articolazioni del potere in provincia (1922–1938)*, Grosseto, Effigi, 2018.
29. D. Tabor, 'Operai in camicia nera? La composizione operaia del fascio di Torino, 1921–1931', *Storia e problemi contemporanei*, 17, 36, 2004, p. 39.

(exile to a remote area of Italy) simply on suspicion of being opposed to the regime or because they had been heard speaking ill of the Duce. The man who called his pig 'Mussolini' (in order to have the satisfaction of shouting 'Mussolini pig' in the fields) was dispatched for five years in short order. *Confino* was a rapid administrative procedure and there was no trial, even though it might cost you several years in some locality far from home. Families of those so exiled were often left destitute.

In short, as in any totalitarian regime, it was difficult—probably impossible—to live a 'normal' life without some reference to the fascist-controlled state machine. Like it or not, it was a machine designed to generate a condition of dependence. Fascism controlled people's lives through violence when necessary but, more effectively in the long run, by an implicit form of intimidation. People were forced to ask, 'What will happen to me (and to my family) if I fall foul of the fascist authorities?' One can sympathize with the man expelled from the Party who pleaded, not to be readmitted to the Party, but 'to be readmitted to life'. The much-proclaimed fascist 'order'—that 'order' that some invoke today—was based to a great extent on discretionary control and the creation of unavoidable dependence, given that some kind of collaboration with the regime was implicit in many situations, even for those hostile to Fascism. It was precisely collaboration of this type that generated the complicity with Fascism that the regime was always trying to engineer. Complicity compelled a grudging acceptance, a grudging recognition of legitimacy. Even anti-fascists would sometimes bow to necessity and put on the black shirt when family or work circumstances left no alternative.

The picture painted so far has reflected the workings of the Party and the fascist-controlled state machine. The role of the police should not be neglected, however. Here it is important to remember that the police were a body of the state, answering to the Ministry of the Interior, and not in any way dependent on the Fascist Party. Mussolini met with his Chief of Police—for most of the *ventennio* Arturo Bocchini—almost every morning in order to review the situation of public order. All the indications are that the police, and the Political Police (formed in 1927) in particular, were very efficient. Bocchini certainly knew his job. His principal task, more than the repression of individual dissent (or the careful watch he kept on 'dissident' fascists), was to prevent the formation of any kind of association of opponents of the regime, and in this he was largely successful. Through the use of spies and informers he was able to curtail anti-fascist activities to a considerable extent and, perhaps more important, through the same methods he managed to spread the fear of denunciation among the general public.

For most people, OVRA—the secret police—remained a mysterious organization (as was intended) and, although in fact directed principally at the battle against the anti-fascists, its 'tentacles' were suspected of extending everywhere. Fear of police informers, of phone-tapping, of censorship of mail grew throughout the twenty years of the regime. People complained that 'the walls have ears'. Strangers in the coffee bar became suspect, therefore. Friends and acquaintances stopped expressing their grievances in public for fear of being overheard by an informer. So successful was the system of control that, at the end of the 1930s, one police informer complained that it was becoming impossible for him to do his job. His targets had simply stopped talking politics in public, in this way, inadvertently, creating what all authoritarian regimes hope to realize—the self-surveilling society which itself checks all expression of criticism of the regime before it arrives at any explicit formulation.[30]

Successful repression, through the police and through the mechanisms conditioning behaviour described above, was the precondition for mobilization in the fascist direction. The transformation of society along fascist lines required first a process of disaggregation of a previous social and political culture and then a cultural reconstruction. The

30. See M. Canali, *Le spie del regime*, Bologna, Il Mulino, 2004; M. Franzinelli, I tentacoli dell'OVRA; M. Franzinelli, *Delatori. Spie e confidenti anonimi. L'arma segreta del regime*, Milan, Mondadori, 2001. Illuminating on the activity of special police corps is V. Coco, *Polizia speciale. Dal fascismo alla repubblica*, Rome-Bari, Laterza, 2017.

police certainly played their part in this process, probably doing their job of repression more effectively than the Party was able to carry out its role of mobilization.

The system described above hardly corresponds to that of a 'benevolent regime'. In fact it bears close similarities with aspects of social control in the Soviet Union, even if the sanctions directed at out-of-order behaviour were obviously very different. Yet, while we have never forgotten the Gulag, the strict social control that was a characteristic of Italian Fascism seems to have been removed from memory. As we have already said, it was a regime of sticks and carrots. The sticks were always obvious, but access to the carrots was conditional; political criteria permeated many important aspects of civilian life and most people had little choice but to try to live according to those criteria. They might find their way around them, as people always do, even in totalitarian regimes, but the conditioning effect of control was always there. This, inevitably, brings us to the thorny question of consensus.

3

Italy

A nation of fascists?

Mass consensus and mass coercion

Life under totalitarian regimes is a subject that has attracted increasing interest over recent decades. How ordinary people adapted to the rigours of domination, what they thought about the regimes, how they obeyed and how they evaded the rules—these are all questions that have stimulated the curiosity of historians.[1] The attitudes of the population of Nazi Germany received attention from the 1970s onwards, with studies of popular opinion which attempted to understand what lay behind the Germans' commitment to Hitler. More recently (in part because of the availability of material) the question of the extent to which communist ideology was accepted and internalized by the Soviet population has produced fascinating studies of life and thought in the Soviet Union, with a continuing process of revision of previously asserted positions. If, in the West, the confrontational ideology of the Cold War prompted people to think that totalitarian domination was based exclusively on indoctrination and coercion, all these studies have painted a different and more complex picture. There was no simple

---

1. Best exemplified in the work of Alf Lüdtke. See, in particular, his edited volume *The History of Everyday Life. Reconstructing Historical Experience and Ways of Life*, Princeton, Princeton University Press, 1995.

and straightforward one-to-one relationship between domination and those dominated.[2]

Few issues have occupied historians of Italian Fascism over the last forty years more than that of the extent of popular consensus for the regime.[3] It is a question that evidently goes beyond the strictly historical problem, because it involves the Italian self-image, what Italians think of their country and of themselves. Were we really *fascists*? And if so, why? Such questions have profound personal and political implications. Here it is necessary to recap very briefly some of the points made in the introductory Chapter 1. As we have seen, the post-war anti-fascist tradition asserted that Italians were, in the main, victims of Fascism and not consenting supporters of the regime. The longevity of the regime was thus ascribed to repression and the impossibility of expressing opposition. Controversy developed when historian Renzo De Felice challenged this orthodoxy in the 1970s, arguing that there had been, not just a consensus, but a 'mass consensus' for Fascism (but only in the years 1929–34, immediately following the Concordat—a detail missed by many of those who embraced the thesis). With this argument he effectively inverted conventional interpretations of the regime. Italians were no longer victims, they were, in a sense, perpetrators; they had been willing accomplices of Mussolini.

The phrase De Felice used—'mass consensus'—was the subject of bitter debate because of its political implications. The Left rejected the idea that a violent and repressive regime could have been generally popular ('ordinary people'—the main supporters of the Left—could not, by definition, have been fascist); the Right, very obviously, took up the new thesis with enthusiasm because popularity (as mass consensus was interpreted) was assumed to be also justification. Rather

2. For a summary of the various debates, see the essays in P. Corner (ed.), *Popular Opinion in Totalitarian Regimes. Fascism, Nazism, Communism*, Oxford, Oxford University Press, 2009. More recently, for a global survey of the question, see Corner and Lim, *The Palgrave Handbook of Mass Dictatorship*.

3. A useful brief summary of the debate up until 2002 can be found in the entry by G. Santomassimo in V. De Grazia and S. Luzzatto (eds), *Dizionario del fascismo*, I, Turin, Einaudi, 2002, pp. 347–52. For other references, see note 5 of Chapter 1.

surprisingly, because of its implications of national responsibility, perhaps even guilt, De Felice's thesis was generally accepted and has become one of the commonplaces of comment on the regime, inducing—as we anticipated in Chapter 1—not consternation and soul-searching on the German model but indulgence, complacency, and a kind of national self-absolution. As if there were no further questions to be answered. As one historian has put it, 'The argument is sterile...because no one any longer denies the involvement of the masses with the regime.'[4] But it is, very obviously, the nature and the extent of that involvement that has to be analysed.

It is worth repeating the reasoning that lies at the heart of this self-absolution because it is central to our argument. It seems to go: If we were all fascists, and if Italians are 'brava gente', that is, by definition, good people, then Fascism cannot have been so bad. It is a reasoning that permits the consolidation of the 'good-natured regime' interpretation of Fascism. Thus we can happily accommodate the dictator who made only one 'mistake'—the alliance with Hitler and entry into the Second World War (but then why make a fuss? we all make mistakes). Berlusconi's rehabilitation of Gianfranco Fini's Movimento Sociale (the neo-fascist movement, later renamed Alleanza Nazionale) in the first half of the 1990s served to consolidate this reading of the past.

This instrumental use of the 'mass consensus' argument hinders rather than helps any attempt at historical reconstruction; it draws a veil over what was an obviously diversified reality. The very complexity of the issue suggests that it is not legitimate to employ the simplistic 'mass consensus' formula in order to pass to a generalized self-absolution in respect of Fascism. Moreover, as we have noted, self-absolution has been followed by removal and amnesia, again impeding further analysis of what went on under the regime. The motives for this amnesia are not difficult to identify. It has been both politically and personally convenient to accept what has now become a kind of comforting

4. S. Colarizi, cited in E. Gentile (ed.), Modernità totalitaria. Il fascismo italiano, Rome-Bari, Laterza, 2008, p. xi.

approach to the fascist past—it is comforting to know that we were all willing passengers in the same boat, even if the boat did eventually run aground. Thus the concept of 'mass consensus' has persuaded people that Fascism can be swept under the carpet and that there are no more questions to be answered. Which is odd. To return once more to the Nazi parallel, consensus for Nazism in Germany raises all sorts of awkward and unpleasant questions; an asserted 'mass consensus' for Fascism in Italy apparently raises none. Germany may have a past that doesn't pass; Italy has a past that—all things considered—seems to present no problems.[5]

'Mass consensus' for Fascism has become one of the great myths regarding the regime. Not because there was no consensus. There was spontaneous and, in certain moments, widespread consensus; there should be no attempt to try to play down the undoubted support for the regime, coming from many directions. There were many 'true believers' in the fascist faith, particularly among the urban petty bourgeoisie and among large and small proprietors in the rural areas. Nationalist and Mazzinian sentiment was strong among the middle and lower middle classes and these undoubtedly responded enthusiastically to the appeal of Fascism. And, if we can now recognize that there was no real threat of a socialist revolution in Italy in the immediate post-war because Italian socialists were divided, badly organized, and without a coherent project, it may not have looked like that to people living through the turmoil of those years. After all, they had images of Moscow and St Petersburg, Berlin, and Vienna before their eyes. In the early years, fear undoubtedly pushed many towards Mussolini.

There *were* fascists, and in large numbers. No one puts this in doubt. Aspects of the regime undoubtedly appealed across the board. Nor should it be forgotten that that most powerful institution, the Catholic Church, did much to bolster the position of the regime, particularly

---

5. For a succinct survey of the German debate, see G. Eley (ed.), *The 'Goldhagen Effect'. History, Memory, Nazism—Facing the German Past*, Ann Arbor, University of Michigan Press, 2000.

in the 1930s after the signature of the Concordat. The Church, itself heavily contaminated by nationalism after the experience of the First World War, was in no sense indifferent to the anti-communist stance of the regime and was itself attempting to come to terms with mass society. In many respects Church and state were parallel rather than competing totalitarianisms.[6] Even the language of the Church moved from being patriotic and religious to being very near to national-fascist, thus coinciding with the language of the fascist faith, which, in a kind of circular process, was itself redolent of the language of the Church. Although he was not typical of all priests, it is difficult to forget Cardinal Schuster blessing the troops leaving for their Ethiopian adventure.

Looked at superficially, the case for mass consensus seems indisputable. However, appearances notwithstanding, a word of caution is due. Perhaps more than a word. As is readily apparent, 'mass consensus' is a blanket concept utilized to cover a very complex question with a single, simplistic, formulation; it suggests a monolithic society, without differentiation, and it operates in terms of black or white. Certainly, areas of consensus can be identified—an overwhelming and generalized consensus not. As in most countries, most ordinary people hated some things, tolerated others, and approved of others at the same time, depending on class, gender, occupation, material circumstances, level of politicization, location, and so on. Given a moment of thought, the many faces of popular opinion are fairly obvious. The job of the historian is to try to assess the relative weights of these attitudes, to try to understand how these attitudes were formed, how they were reflected in behaviour, and, of course, how they changed in the course of time. These are the questions that have to be answered and the answers are rarely crystal clear. Inevitably, it is hard to assess opinions under regimes that suppress the expression of opinion and conclusions can

6. See L. Ceci, 'La Chiesa e il fascismo. Nuovi paradigmi e nuove fonti', in *Studi storici*, 1, 2014, pp. 123–37.

never be more than approximate. Ambiguity and ambivalence play a role that make firm judgements difficult.[7]

In any analysis of consensus we have to start from problems of definition (what does consensus mean in a repressive state where dissent is punished?) and continue with questions relating to the interpretation of the source material available (what to believe, what not to believe). In fact, a closer analysis of the situation in the 1920s and 1930s indicates that the consensus thesis—as it is generally understood today—requires considerable qualification. So considerable, in fact, as to make its acceptance highly problematic. Even a rapid reconsideration suggests that something does not square. If everyone was agreed about their support for the regime, if there was a mass consensus, then why was it necessary to construct the vast repressive mechanism we have outlined in the previous chapter? Why did Mussolini meet with his Chief of Police every morning to discuss questions of public order? Why were OVRA and the Political Police created? Why invent the Special Tribunal for crimes against the fascist state? What were the militiamen of the MVSN supposed to do all day? Why was blackshirt violence still common at the end of the 1930s? After all, even De Felice noted very widespread police activity in the period 1929–34 (that is, in his period of 'mass consensus').[8] Somehow or other we seem to have mass consensus and widespread dissent at the same time—a paradox that needs to be explained.

In fact, the thesis of 'mass consensus' does not stand up to close examination if it is taken to mean that there was a generalized popular consensus for Fascism throughout the two decades of fascist rule, that there were no variations in the level of support in different periods, and, above all, that lack of open protest is an indication of consensus.

7. On the methodological difficulties of assessing popular opinion, see Corner (ed.), *Popular Opinion in Totalitarian Regimes*, introduction. On the problems presented in assessing ambiguity and ambivalence, see K. Ferris, *Everyday Life in Fascist Venice*, London, Palgrave Macmillan, 2012.

8. R. De Felice, *Mussolini il Duce. Gli anni del consenso 1929–36*, Turin, Einaudi, 1974, p. 83, where he refers to an average of 20,000 police actions against opponents of the regime in the course of an average week.

It is in this last respect that we have a clear methodological problem. From what we have said so far in the previous chapter about violence and heavy social control, it should be clear that the free expression of opinion or the free decision about personal behaviour was possible only within very closely determined limits. As with any authoritarian regime, and even more so in a regime that considered itself totalitarian, you lived within a context of control and it was impossible not to be aware of this conditioning context. Conditioning meant being conscious of limits that should not be exceeded and one of the limits was certainly that of protest or expressions of discontent. Hardly surprisingly, this conditioning effect is reflected in the written evidence available to the historian. While we can find with ease diaries of supporters of the regime, of those who express unconditional support for the Duce, there are far fewer written testimonies of opposition. It was simply not wise to put such thoughts to paper.[9]

In this context it is important to remember that the very strong left-wing subculture expressed in the immediate first post-war did not disappear overnight with the arrival of the regime. In many places, particularly in the north of Italy, it was defused but remained present, without open expression, only to re-emerge, often with a vengeance, after 1943. Luisa Passerini's study of Turin workers in the interwar period suggests strongly that those who had been convinced socialists in 1920–1 were unlikely to be enthusiastic members of the PNF (Partito Nazionale Fascista) in 1930. Some kind of reluctant complicity was more probable—'a social acceptance' of the situation is how Passerini puts it—because class sentiment was too strong to have disappeared so quickly. As we have seen, complicity with the regime was unavoidable for many if they wanted to work. One worker described

9. See C. Duggan, *Fascist Voices. An Intimate History of Mussolini's Italy*, London, Bodley Head, 2013. The study charts, through the use of letters and personal diaries, the enthusiasm and almost religious devotion that Fascism engendered in some Italians. It should be said, to inject a word of caution, that an analysis of the authors of the forty or so diaries used in Duggan's survey shows them to be written, unsurprisingly, largely by middle and lower middle class people—usually seen as the principal constituency of the regime.

his own position in respect of the Party succinctly, 'tesserato sì, fassista no' ('enrolled yes, fascist no').[10] Fascist mobilization, by putting the crowds in the public square, hid this fact from view, emphasizing visible unity of intent and apparent choral consensus for the regime. The world was made to look as though there was no opposition. This was important; it suggested legitimacy of rule. Moreover, the appearance of unity might persuade those who continued to oppose it that it was they, and not the fascists, who were really out of step with the times. If you can't beat them, join them, is an adage that sometimes seems to make sense.[11]

In the circumstances of repressive dictatorship, lack of open and vocal protest can hardly be interpreted as 'consensus', at least in the usual meaning of the word. The repressive mechanisms of the regime worked in such a way as to make it appear (to Italians just as much as to foreign onlookers) that there was a generalized consensus. And the regime did everything it could to make it look as though there was a mass consensus; the carefully orchestrated mass demonstrations were an essential legitimizing operation. Delirious crowds appeared to make Mussolini a 'legitimate' dictator. This was important for the regime in its populist stance—Mussolini always claimed to be speaking on behalf of 'the Italian people'; it was always 'the people' who would ratify his actions.

However, the appearances of unity and enthusiasm may have belied the reality. The 'true believers' there were, certainly, but what of the rest—those who toed the fascist line because of coercion and constriction? Can their silence be interpreted as consensus? Very evidently not. Any consensus thus demonstrated was always demonstrated within the wider context of intimidation and coercion; it was consensus *within* coercion. If anything, coercion was intended to establish a carefully

10. L. Passerini, *Torino operaio e fascismo. Una storia orale*, Rome-Bari, Laterza, 1984.
11. See P. Corner, 'Plebiscites in fascist Italy. National unity and the importance of the appearance of unity', in R. Jessen and H. Richter (eds), *Voting for Hitler and Stalin. Elections under 20th Century Dictatorships*, Frankfurt am Main, Campus Verlag, 2011, pp. 173–85.

controlled path along which people would move towards acceptance of the regime, in large part because of enforced complicity with the regime. For this reason coercion and consensus cannot be seen as opposites; they exist together, as two sides of the same repressive coin.

Deductions made on the basis of a supposedly spontaneous and continuous 'mass consensus' fail to acknowledge this connection. A possible comparison, which may help to illustrate better the situation, could be with the organization of popular support under certain of the Soviet satellite regimes in the 1960s and 1970s, where the same flag-waving, cheering, mass demonstrations could be witnessed, supposedly confirming mass enthusiasm for the regimes, but where—as is now well known—participation was largely an obligatory ritual which did not involve any deep commitment to communist values. It was part of the communist package and was lived and accepted as such; you went to the demonstration in the morning and you told anti-communist jokes in the afternoon.[12]

In fascist Italy unavoidable dependence and obligatory collaboration were reinforced by a further factor—a factor that made its presence felt more as the regime progressed. This was the absence of alternatives; not only in the sense described above—the unavoidable contact with a single authority—but because the regime effectively closed the door on possibilities other than Fascism. 'There was nothing else' is a common refrain among those who attempted, in later years, to explain an eventual allegiance to Fascism. Other political systems were condemned out of hand and information about them severely restricted. Certainly the Catholic Church offered a possible refuge, but the alliance between Church and a kind of clerico-fascism during the 1930s made that refuge no more than partial. Fascism pervaded everywhere. The regime preached its own exclusive virtues from

12. For this kind of behaviour, see J. Plamper, 'Beyond binaries? Popular opinion in Stalinism', in Corner (ed.), *Popular Opinion in Totalitarian Regimes*. See also, for the attitudes of the last Soviet generation, A. Yurchak, *Everything was Forever, until it was No More*, Princeton, Princeton University Press, 2005.

elementary school onwards; infants were taught to love the Duce and to raise their right arms in salute almost as soon as they could walk.

This enforced closure in respect of alternatives is one of the hall-marks of totalitarianism. People are left with no other choice than to accept the reality represented by the regime—to the extent that, after time, they become unaware that the possibility of choice exists. For some—particularly for those who grew up in Italy under these conditions—the so-called 'second generation'—this could not be without effect; a certain kind of conformism was built into the system and was difficult to evade. At the end of the 1930s, for university students enrolled in the *Gruppi universitari fascisti*—a very small minority among young Italians, it must be remembered[13]—what certainly was consensus was a product of a situation in which it appeared that, as many have subsequently testified, 'there were no alternatives'. For these, Fascism was the norm, the only reality available, and—a not unimportant consideration—the only path to social promotion. Much suggests that, at least as far as a very restricted social group represented by students goes, and despite the irritation with many aspects of the regime expressed by members of that group, the insistent messages of the regime had their effect.[14]

But perhaps the best example of 'enforced consensus', as expressed by the general public, is provided by a close look at fascist demonstra-tions, such as those in Piazza Venezia in Rome, when Mussolini would appear to the cheering crowds to make his 'historic' announcements. The films of these events, produced by the Istituto Luce, were them-selves designed to be propaganda for the regime, to be shown in the more remote areas of Italy. They showed such delirium and enthusi-asm that few would ever think to deny the popular support for the

13. In 1939 around 100,000 among four million young people. On the members of GUF (*gufini*) see S. Duranti, *Lo spirito gregario*, Rome, Donzelli, 2008; L. La Rovere, *Storia dei GUF*, Turin, Bollati Boringhieri, 2003.

14. Studies of these students have been cited as evidence that 'true believers' did exist and that the process of 'internalization' of fascist ideology had taken place. While this may be true for a part of this very small minority of young Italians, their complaints at the end of the 1930s that many, particularly working class, Italians did not 'know' Fascism does suggest that there was no generalized mass consensus for the regime.

regime. Even today, when shown on television, they invite the same uncritical reading. However, police and Fascist Party documents provide a slightly different picture. The 'spontaneous' enthusiasm of fascist rallies—the impressively named *adunate oceaniche* ('oceanic demonstrations')—was carefully constructed for weeks before the rally took place. In the days before a demonstration the local party offices would receive a convocation card for all those for whom the offices were responsible and the cards would be distributed to everyone who was expected to attend the rally. Names and numbers were on these cards. On the day of the demonstration, the cards had to be handed in to fascist officials seated at tables set up at the entrances to the square. Thus, people were counted, absentees noted, and those absent were subject to severe sanctions. Moreover the rallies were very carefully choreographed. Those known to be in favour of the regime were arranged at the front in order that their support could be filmed and noted; those less warmly disposed towards the regime had a place much further back. In fact, in many demonstrations police informers would report that the mood at the back of the crowd was anything but enthusiastic. People complained that it was boring, that it was all a waste of time. One informer's report on the rally of 2 October 1935, when Mussolini announced the invasion of Ethiopia, quoted a fascist who said to his friends that he was afraid Mussolini would interpret obligatory presence in the square as an indication of support for the war, which it was not. On the same occasion a fascist official quite rightly made the observation that obligatory presence at the demonstration was a mistake because it made it impossible to gauge the level of genuine support for the regime. It was, in any case—he went on—too easy to interpret the enforced enthusiasm of the moment as denoting a lasting fascist conviction. The sentiment was echoed by a foreign journalist who wrote of the Italians as a 'population condemned to enthusiasm'.[15]

---

15. For a more detailed account, see P. Corner, 'Italian fascism. Organization, enthusiasm, opinion', *Journal of Modern Italian Studies*, 15, 2010.

Here, very evidently, was 'coerced consensus'. You went to the rally because you had to; you went because it was in your interest to do so and you behaved as if you were a loyal fascist. Almost all dictatorships produce the same kind of behaviour in the population; the 'as if' factor is always evident. So much depended on behaving 'as if' you were a loyal supporter of the regime.[16] The great Italian historian and politician Gaetano Salvemini recorded an excellent example of this kind of behaviour in his memoirs. As recounted to him by a union organizer in Alessandria, a group of fifty workers on a train, going to work in nearby France, all wore the fascist badge prominently on their jackets (teams of workers such as these would have been selected by some fascist-orientated employment office). Once past the frontier, however, and assured—twice—that they were outside Italian jurisdiction, all removed the badge immediately, 'cursing [the badges] as only Tuscans know how to curse and stamping on them'.[17]

Further examples of this kind of obligatory observance of the outward forms are not difficult to find. As a leatherworker from Certaldo, near Florence, put it in later years, making very clear the link between political obedience, work, and food: 'The majority came to terms with the situation. They went to the fascist rallies because they said, "At least I get to work and eat". They knew how to lie.' The threat of fascist reprisals could also be directed at a person's family and used as an instrument of blackmail, as with one young man who resisted the local fascist leader's order to go to a fascist rally in Florence: 'I had never taken part when they did their festivities. I told him that I wasn't going to Florence. Then the secretary of the *fascio*, Vichi, said to me, "If you don't come to Florence I'll arrest your father and your mother". I got my clothes together to go to Florence.'[18] Other

16. On the 'as if' factor, see L. Wedeen, *Ambiguities of Domination. Politics, Rhetoric, and Symbols in Contemporary Syria*, Chicago, University of Chicago Press, 1999.
17. G. Salvemini, *Memorie e soliloqui. Diario 1922–25*, Bologna, Il Mulino, 2001, p. 402. The same organizer told Salvemini that all kiln workers in his area had to declare loyalty to Fascism if they wanted to avoid being beaten up or having to 'see their union leaders killed'.
18. Quoted in F. Rossi (ed.), *Certaldo negli anni del fascismo. Un comune toscano fra le due guerre (1919–1940)*, Milan, La Pietra, 1986. p. 213.

accounts speak of workers being warned that their behaviour at rallies would be carefully monitored from the sidelines.

The role of the Party

The task of mobilizing support for the regime in the provinces—of organizing consensus—lay with the Fascist Party, the PNF—a capillary network of organizations intended to purvey the policies of the centre to the provinces and from the provincial centres to the provincial periphery. This was a part of the centralizing thrust of fascist policy, the attempt to make sure that what was decided in Rome was understood and obeyed throughout the country.[19] Local interests, always very strong in Italy, were finally to be subordinated to national values. As a transmission belt the PNF had a crucial role in developing that kind of 'coerced consensus' we have noted above, and, in many areas, it undoubtedly carried out this function; the long lists of activities, ranging from picnics, tug of war contests, cycle rides, to target shooting and canoeing, that provincial fascist federations would send in to the central office in Rome, attested to a high level of activity. The operation of the various youth groups—Balilla, Avanguardisti, and so on—were also very much to the fore. And the Party extended its control, in one way or another, over much of the increasingly extensive local administration, including welfare.

Whether this control and all this activity did translate into 'consensus' remains doubtful, however. There is a wealth of evidence in the archives to suggest that, in many provincial contexts, the PNF failed to function as intended. Various factors contributed to this failure. Perhaps the most important was that, in his circular of 1927, Mussolini made it clear that the ultimate authority in the provincial context was the prefect, appointed by the Ministry of the Interior, and not the

---

19. For an examination of the social composition of the 'new directing class' and the workings of the PNF, see G. Melis, *La macchina imperfetta. Immagini e realtà dello Stato fascista*, Bologna, Il Mulino, 2019, ch. 2.

local fascist boss (the *segretario federale* or simply *federale*), something that did not go down well with many fascist provincial leaders who imagined that they had 'carried out the revolution' in order to be free of the dictates of the prefect, seen by them to be the epitome of the old liberal order. Provincial leaders felt the ground being removed from under their feet and often resisted the implications of the circular, to the extent that, in point of fact, the subordination of the Party to the prefect was never fully observed by many local bosses, who, in their local contexts, continued to behave as though it was they—the fascists—who commanded. The inevitable tensions that arose between state authority and fascist pretensions to control were to characterize the history of many provinces in the late 1920s and the 1930s, creating a short-circuit in the provincial chain of command which often impeded any effective mobilizing activity. At times, a similar conflict would develop between the commanders of the local MVSN militia and the *Carabinieri*—once again essentially a conflict between Party and state.[20]

The damage created by conflicts of competence was compounded by other divisions within the fascist movement. Local leaders—the *ras* as they were known—were often people who, from nothing, had risen to almost absolute power in their provinces during the period immediately before the March on Rome. Many of them intended to hold on to that power; 'Rome can do what it likes. Here I command' was a common attitude. Such leaders usually had local competitors, equally convinced that they had earned the right to rewards. As a

---

20. The exact nature of the subordination of the Fascist Party to the state is the subject of discussion. Certainly the Party was intended to be the backbone of the fascist movement in the provinces and was far from being just a passive instrument of central government. At the same time, this 'backbone' functioned badly for a whole series of reasons, producing deleterious results for the entire movement. For the malfunctioning of the Party in the provinces, see P. Corner, *The Fascist Party and Popular Opinion in Mussolini's Italy*, Oxford, Oxford University Press, 2012. For a more general consideration of the relationship between state and Party, see M. Palla, 'Lo Stato-partito', in M. Palla (ed.), *Lo Stato fascista*, Milan, La Nuova Italia, 2001, pp. 7–8 and, more recently, L. Di Nucci, *Lo Stato-partito del fascismo. Genesi, evoluzione e crisi 1919–1943*, Bologna, Il Mulino, 2009.

consequence rivalries between local fascists—some loyal to one leader, some to another—produced situations in which the local federation rapidly became paralysed. After 1925, the contests between rival groups—on occasions they ended up shooting at each other—became one of the hallmarks of provincial Fascism, with old blackshirts contesting the rise of younger people, the old elite of the towns resisting the pressures of new faces coming from the hinterland, radical fascists denouncing the moderate tones of their more conservative colleagues—and so on. In what was, very obviously, a contest for local power rather than a genuine contest of principle, provincial Fascism often lost sight of what the regime was supposed to represent, with a consequent loss of reputation. This, inevitably, had an effect on popular opinion. As informers reported to Rome, the scene in many provinces was unedifying to say the least, and was reflected in the fact that many able people were being careful to steer clear of having anything to do with local administration because, in the circumstances of provincial career-ism and infighting, they were reluctant to assume any kind of respon-sibility. A consensus for the regime was hardly being constructed around this kind of chaos. One notes a singular absence of the sense of 'national community' that the Nazi movement was so successful in propagating.

A further factor contributed to the difficulties the PNF faced in mobilizing support for the regime, and that was corruption.[21] This was, in part, a reflection of the poor quality of many provincial fascist leaders. Some were undoubtedly serious and honest people—Renzo Ravenna in Ferrara was just such a person[22]—but others left a lot to be desired. As the regime progressed, opinion turned against PNF administration. Local fascist officials were often thought to be corrupt, using their public authority for private benefit. Here we see a pattern common to totalitarian regimes. It was one of the paradoxes of

21. M. Palla and P. Giovannini (eds), *Il fascismo dalle mani sporche. Dittatura, corruzione, affarismo*, Rome-Bari, Laterza, 2019.
22. I. Pavan, *Il podestà ebreo. La storia di Renzo Ravenna tra fascismo e leggi razziali*, Rome-Bari, Laterza, 2006.

totalitarianism, visible in other regimes, that the process supposed to incorporate the private within the 'total' public sphere, thus eliminating the private, in fact favoured the privatization of many of the functions of the public realm. Control was in the hands of those who should have been controlled, hence it was largely absent. Given the way in which the fascists had gained power—the 'here *I* control every-thing' attitude typical of the provincial fascist bosses—this privatiza-tion of authority, with its accompanying corruption, was hardly surprising.[23]

Corruption among politicians is in no sense limited to totalitarian regimes, of course, but it seems to have been particularly rife in Italy under Fascism. During the 1930s, and more particularly in the second half of the decade, with the increasing stagnation of the Party, there was a general perception at popular level that a 'new caste' had been created by the regime—an arrogant caste more interested in exploit-ing positions of authority than in following the dictates of Rome. The 'Napoleonic uniforms' and 'gladiatorial poses' of provincial leaders were much derided, but what attracted particular attention was exag-gerated lifestyle and mysterious sources of sudden wealth. As one man (subsequently arrested) put it: 'the quality necessary for high political or administrative office is that of refined delinquency'. Another lamented that 'never has bourgeois Italy been as corrupt as it is today'.[24] It is around this perception that the 'If only Mussolini knew...' illusion developed, people ingenuously believing that the Duce had no idea of what was going on.[25]

Another aspect, not, of course, unknown today and perhaps more akin to cronyism than to direct corruption, was the use of position by

---

23. For a parallel process of privatization of authority, see J. T. Gross, *Revolution from Abroad. The Soviet Conquest of Poland's Western Ukraine and Western Bielorussia*, Princeton, Princeton University Press, 2002, ch. 3.

24. Corner, *Fascist Party*, pp. 208, 238.

25. It is significant that it was the discrediting of political parties in Italy in 1992–3, above all around the scandal of 'mani pulite' ('clean hands'), that persuaded some people to look back to Fascism as a period of honesty and integrity—the present affecting the perception of the past.

prominent fascists in order to find lucrative posts in the governing boards of banks and private companies. Many high-level fascist officials enjoyed several such posts at the same time. The French historian Didier Musdielak has documented very scrupulously a whole series of such connections, with people known to be near to the centres of command in Rome receiving large sums—often many. hundreds of thousands of lire—simply to be part of the governing board and, presumably, use their influence in Rome when necessary.[26] This kind of operation was the subject of increasing criticism during the 1930s and there are indications, from the reports of informers, that, towards the end of the decade, there was massive popular irritation about the self-interested activities of the 'new caste'. Accusations that fascist officials were making money 'by the spadeful' were common, sometimes even from disgusted fascists. The 'public' area of fascist administration—that area so much expanded by the regime—was increasingly brought into disrepute; some people were simply getting too rich too quickly.

None of this was conducive to the formation of a spontaneous mass consensus for the regime. In many provinces, the paralysis of the Party, together with the perception of arrogance and corruption within the Party, turned opinion away from the regime. By the end of the 1930s there was exhaustion at continuous pointless obligatory activities, which people were increasingly deserting, and mounting complaints about shortages and the cost of living. The extent to which the difficult material conditions of daily life translated into political opposition may be questioned—the regime ensured that there was really nowhere to go—but the widespread grumbling did nothing to help fascist popularity. Increasingly, comments reported by informers showed that people were beginning to question the behaviour of the regime, particularly in the sense that, while the regime consistently exaggerated its performance, in reality it had failed to keep its promises.

26. D. Musiedlak, *Lo stato fascista e la sua classe politica 1922–1943*, Bologna, Il Mulino, 2003. The move to prevent the accumulation of various lucrative positions (1933) remained largely without effect.

Informers noted that people spoke all the time about 'they'—those responsible for hardship—and that by this they meant the fascists. Identification with the regime was at a very low ebb.

The Party was unable to come to terms with these problems. Indeed, it was considered to be itself one of the principal problems people had to deal with. As with Nazism, where the 'little Hitlers' were loathed, so too were the arrogant and corrupt 'little Mussolinis', it was the charisma of the leader that kept things together. 'Mussolini yes, Fascism no' might sum up a widespread sentiment in the later part of the 1930s—with its obvious corollary that the regime would not outlive its leader.

As long as admiration for Mussolini continued to keep many within the fascist fold, the Party had to be tolerated, but when—as we shall see—Mussolini's reputation began to lose its shine towards the end of the 1930s, the weaknesses of party organization and the problems generated by their loss of esteem came into the open. Hitler, still on the ascendant in the 1930s, could ride out the problems within the provincial Nazi Party; Mussolini, on the decline after more than a decade in power, faced a more difficult task. As doubts increased about his 'intuition', his control of the international situation, and even his state of health, the capacity for 'coerced consensus' began to waver. By 1939 even fascists were beginning to talk about what would happen 'after Fascism'—a serious alarm signal for a would-be totalitarian regime. This was very different from the situation in Germany, despite the parallels in local party unpopularity. In Italy a declining movement was combined with a declining leader and an enforced 'consensus' was never going to stem this decline.

All of this suggests that the depth of 'fascistization' of at least a considerable part of the population had been limited and that the objective of subsuming society into the state—the 'Everything within the state' objective—had not been achieved. Corrupt officials and conflicts of competence apart, this failure was built into the project. In a sense fascist thought rejected politics as such; it was the Duce who decided everything, and government was there simply for administration through an expanded bureaucracy and an overseeing structure of corporations. Politics was to be replaced by administration. Thus we find a newly appointed local fascist leader arriving at his provincial destination proclaiming 'No politics, no cannibalism'; politics meant conflict and division—fascist 'eating' fascist—and was therefore to be avoided.[27] As a consequence, the fascist slogan 'believe, obey, fight' was never accompanied, for the mass of the people, with the imperative 'think', and, as historian De Felice (allegedly the prophet of the 'mass consensus' thesis) has insisted, this produced widespread disgust with politics and a growing depoliticization.[28] People either lost interest or simply avoided politics.

Much of the very considerable 'political' activity of the regime was often essentially a façade, therefore—a fact widely recognized at the end of the 1930s when fascists themselves began to complain that activities were no more than people going through the motions, simply the exhibition of appearances, with the pointless parading of medals and colourful uniforms—all with no real significance.[29] What sometimes looked like 'mass consensus' was no more than this—enforced acceptance and ritualized regimentation without any genuine commitment.

This was hardly the imagined 'mass consensus' utilized by some today to paint a picture of a Fascism that was 'not so bad' in order to generate a spirit of indulgence towards the regime. Rather it was a situation that suggests an existential emptiness (since described as such in novels and memoirs)—the result of a long period of repression which had seen only rare moments of real stimulus. In the end, far from mobilizing the masses, totalitarianism had a dulling effect. As Masha Gessen has noted in respect of the Soviet Union, communism

27. S. Lupo, Il fascismo. La politica di un regime totalitario, Rome, Donzelli, 2000, p. 24.
28. 'Beneath the appearance of extreme politicisation of the masses, an ever more marked and real depoliticisation of society [was taking place] which led to an ever more accentuated separation from, and an ever-increasing disdain for the PNF and...to a general disgust for politics as such'; De Felice, Mussolini il Duce, vol. 2, p. 221.
29. Corner, Fascist Party, p. 220.

tended, in the long run, to produce an *Uomo sovieticus* who was anything but the dynamic New Man envisaged in the early days of the revolution. Instead he was passive, conformist, and without initiative.[30] The most common attitude in respect of government was simply to avoid politics and let someone else get on with the job. By the end of the 1930s many Italians responded to Fascism in the same way. Like their Soviet counterparts, they shunned political activity. It was a further paradox of totalitarianism that, when everything became political because the regime purported to determine everything for its subjects, the result was massive depoliticization.

30. M. Gessen, *The Future is History. How Totalitarianism Reclaimed Russia*, New York, Riverhead, 2017.

4

Things were better when HE was in charge ...

One of the more persistent myths relating to the fascist period is that people lived well under the regime—'things were better when HE was around'.[1] It is a myth that generates a predisposition to authority and one that we have already encountered in respect of other dictatorships. Nostalgia for past communist regimes often looks back to a 'phantom utopia'. A recent, and classic, example of the force of nostalgia comes from Poland, with the production of 'Edward Gierek traditional sausages', said to 'recapture the taste of sausages enjoyed by our parents when things were better'. In Italy the illusion rests on a few commonplaces. A certain popular memory tries to remind us that, under Fascism, there was discipline, rectitude, order, and security—and there was justice. Rough justice, perhaps, but at any rate criminals got their deserts. You knew where you were; you knew that someone was in control and that HE was looking out for you. Moreover—the story goes—personal security was enhanced by a sense of national direction, by the knowledge that Italy was finally respected abroad. In contrast to the present, it was a world in which things were still in place and you could look forward to your pension (which, of course, Mussolini invented) in tranquillity.

---

1. One of the more ridiculous orders of Party secretary Achille Starace was that all written references to Mussolini were to be made in capital letters.

Nostalgia generally tends to paint the past with gold and the memory of Fascism is no exception. It was, after all, a period that saw many new and exciting developments, which, if not inventions of the time, saw their first more widespread diffusion in the interwar years. The radio, the cinema, the telephone, a limited level of motorization, the expansion of leisure activities—these were all aspects of a late and slightly uncertain entry into the habits and artefacts characteristic of a consumer society. Even if in Italy that kind of society was very slow in coming, horizons undoubtedly widened for many. And in fact we remember certain of the novelties of the period with pleasure. The songs, the cars, the fashions—they seem to belong to a past innocence which has subsequently been lost.

Yet the warm glow of nostalgia should be seen for what it is— nostalgia and nothing more. Again, it is based on a vision of the regime that removes the negative aspects and accentuates what seems more positive. And it ascribes what seems more positive to the operation of Fascism. In this context, and before going any further, it is wise to remember that the regime did everything it could to glorify its supposed achievements and to relate all changes to the regime itself. Almost everything that happened in Italy over the course of twenty years was put down to the genius of the Duce; fascist propaganda emphasized this continuously. For instance, the expansion of bureaucracy with a message of increased state intervention in the lives of much of the population was a novelty which people were told to associate with an all-caring fascist state and with a fascist leader who loved his people. In the same way the much-trumpeted 'realizations' of the 1930s—public buildings, new towns, new roads, reclaimed marshes—were always 'fascist realizations'. For this reason people were required to give thanks to the genius of Mussolini, whose generous and paternal influence was said to permeate all aspects of public life. Here the reader will have a strong sense of *dejà vu*; the overseeing, paternal dictator is a trope with which we are very familiar from other regimes. In Italy it was certainly not without effect. Propaganda undoubtedly convinced many Italians (and many foreigners) that Italy was at last on the move, thanks to the beneficial impact of the new politics.

Much of this propaganda seems to have filtered through to the present day. It is as if, in the light of today's many difficulties and with the benefit of hindsight, the fascist period now seems one in which things were better, that there were, as the phrase goes, 'many good things' to look back on. However, this persistent vision of an ever-present and usually successful regime raises two very important methodological points. The first—perhaps the more important—is that it is a mistake to attribute everything that changed during the course of the 1920s and 1930s to the regime. Which is to say that, despite the boasting of the regime, not all that happened under Fascism happened because of Fascism. The regime did not exist in a void, nor did it come into existence by filling a void; the context in which the regime operated—that of a slowly emerging mass, increasingly industrialized society—required a change in the role of the state and determined much of what was done. And, if there were pretensions to totalitarian control, in point of fact many institutions and organizations preserved a degree of autonomy and could pursue their own directives without much interference from the regime. Giovanni Agnelli paid lip-service to Mussolini but, when it came to running the Fiat motor company, he went his own way. This may seem obvious, but, in a chapter that deals with social and economic issues, it is essential to remember that social and economic change has many causes, not all of them related to the precise conditions of the political regime of the time. A case in point is the great increase in male suicides between 1925 and 1935. Clearly not all Italians were happy, but whether this was related to Fascism, to the effects of the war, or to the economic difficulties of the period is impossible to tell.[2]

This can be appreciated better in the light of the second point, which is that what happened during the 1920s and 1930s within Italy

2. R. S. Somogyi and S. Somogyi, *Il suicidio in Italia dal 1864 ad oggi*, Milan, Edizioni Kappa, 1995.

should be compared with what happened in other countries of Europe, where many of the same changes also took place. Many of those phenomena associated with modernization were common, a fact that suggests that it is not legitimate to associate them exclusively with the political regime of Italy at that time. Without inquiring too much into what might have been—the rather unprofitable counter-factual approach—we should remember that it is not as though, without a fascist regime, nothing would have changed within Italy. History would not have been put on hold for twenty years. International comparison leads us to think, rather, that it is necessary to ask whether the regime aided or hindered these common processes, whether Fascism represented a regime really conducive to modernization, as it claimed to be. In some respects it is less a question of what was done— any Italian government of the time might have done many of the same things—but how it was done, for whom and to whom, at what cost, and—above all—why. If we fail to understand the 'why', we will be constantly looking at means and not at ends.

The social priorities of Fascism

Changes in social and economic conditions are easier to understand if we look first at those priorities that underlay the operation of the regime. To some extent this looks at the question, why? As is well known, fascist ideology depended heavily on an extreme nationalism—some have described it as ultranationalism—which meant, logically, that at the centre of fascist thinking was the nation, which found its expression in the state.[3] This was evident from the very beginnings of the movement. The extreme violence aimed at the socialists was justified by the blackshirts on the grounds that they, the socialists, were 'anti-national' and had, on occasions, derided the sacrifices of the great

---

3. 'Ultranationalism' is the favourite term of Roger Griffin in *The Nature of Fascism*, London, Pinter, 1991.

national effort of the First World War. What was, in effect, the sacralization of the state on the part of the fascists determined in large part
its social and economic priorities; the ultimate motive for any policy
or decision was that of the strengthening and reinforcing of the state.
And the strong state—this was the important point—was the socially
cohesive state, with the population moving as one in support of the
revolutionary and expansionist national effort. Mussolini's dictum,
'Everything within the state, nothing outside the state, nothing against
the state', expressed this idea very succinctly.

Much of fascist thinking was based on the conviction that the
activities of political parties were divisive and corrupt and did no
more than hinder national progress. Thus, the pluralism of an increasingly democratic nature seen in Italy in the immediate post-war was
judged to be politically damaging and detrimental to Italy's interests,
destroying the essential unity of the state. To realize the fascist revolution, to transform society, the new mass society had to be controlled
and disciplined. With the March on Rome, but more particularly with
the repressive actions and the legislation following 3 January 1925,[4]
the projects aimed at the expansion of a liberal democracy gave way
to those favouring the construction of an organic state, with, as the
guiding principle, the nation-state unified around a single party and a
single leader. The organic state—a concept that owed much to ideas
developed in the decades before the First World War, but found its
renewed inspiration in the experience of the war and of a perceived
(if not real) national unity during the conflict—required that the individual should abandon personal interest and identify fully with the
state. As Emilio Gentile has put it, the fascists aimed at the politicization of civil society 'not in order to realize the formation of autonomous beings but [to realize] the total dedication of the individual and
the masses to the state and to the strength of the nation'.[5]

4. The moment when Mussolini assumed full responsibility for the murder of Matteotti
   and, at the same time, announced a massive programme of repression of all opposition
   parties; usually seen as the beginning of the regime.
5. E. Gentile, *La via italiana al totalitarismo*, Rome-Bari, Laterza, 2002 (1st edition 1999), p. 187.

But what precisely was the state? For the fascists, the state was identified with the government and, increasingly, with the head of government. Fascist ideologues, such as Paolo Orano, even arrived at the point of arguing that the state was embodied in the person of the Duce, and that the function of the state was simply to put into effect his directives.

The Sicilian philosopher Giovanni Gentile theorized a kind of individual 'internalization' of the objectives of the state, producing a total commitment on the part of the individual to those objectives. This was not so much anti-individualism as redefining the function of the individual and removing what the fascist theorist considered to be the divisive and deleterious effects of individualism. The fascist state was to be a fusion of society and state, in which civil society was subsumed in the state, thus realizing the 'total' state. As such it was to be the solution to the persistent Italian problem of acute tension between the masses and the elites, and, in a wider sense, between the masses and authority; conflict was to be replaced by a 'totalitarian' collaboration.[6] Class divisions would not so much cease to exist; they would become irrelevant within the grander national scheme of hierarchy and discipline.

We are accustomed to think of the word 'totalitarian' exclusively in Cold War terms of repression and control; Winston Smith and the Thought Police of Orwell's *1984* are never very far from our mind. But it is important to understand that, in the eyes of any totalitarian theorist, repression and control were a means to an end, and that end was the integration of society with the state. Control—through repression of dissent, destruction of political alternatives, pressure of propaganda—was necessary in order to force people to adopt the totalitarian frame of mind (this would be the job of the PNF). In this

6. For an illuminating analysis of the priorities of Fascism, see P. Costa, 'Lo stato totalitario. Un campo semantico nella giurisprudenza del Fascismo', *Quaderni fiorentini per la storia del pensiero giuridico moderno*, 28, 1999, pp. 61–174.

way the fascist New Man would be created.[7] This was not seen as manipulation of the masses; it was education, formation, and—above all—transformation. Popular consensus for Fascism would result from this process and this consensus was important because it was the visible expression of the unity of society and the ethical state.

Because they worked towards this fusion, hierarchy and discipline within that society were essential elements of the state so formed. Popular representation, as, for example, through parliament, was obviously to be discarded, in part because it suggested a different source of legitimacy, but principally because it would reflect a variety of differing interests in society, challenging its integrity. Fascist anti-parliamentarianism was based on this critical position and it was for this reason that elections, even within the Fascist Party structure, were anathema. Nonetheless, the people were to participate because the concept of hierarchy envisaged a role for everyone within the state— some with a more important role, some less. Hierarchy became a keyword of the regime, therefore, organizing society and effecting participation in a way that neither capitalism nor socialism was able to do. It opened the door to the theoretical 'Third Way' in which the 'objective' agencies and institutions of the state were married with the 'subjective' commitment of the individual to that state.

The corporations—an aspect of Fascism that greatly interested foreign observers—fitted into this scheme in the sense that they—the corporations—were to represent the organizational structure that would permit the nation to surmount the conflicts generated by the processes of production.[8] Whereas, prior to Fascism, workers and bosses had had conflicting interests, with the establishment of the corporations the defining philosophy was to become collaboration, with

7. For a series of interesting essays, see P. Bernhard and L. Klinkhammer (eds), *L'uomo nuovo del Fascismo. La costruzione di un progetto totalitario*, Rome, Viella, 2017.
8. On the corporative state, see Mariuccia Salvati, 'The long history of corporativism in Italy. A question of culture or economics?', *Contemporary European History*, 2, 2006; A. Gagliardi, *Il corporativismo fascista*, Rome-Bari, Laterza, 2010 and G. Santomassimo, *La terza via fascista. Il mito del corporativismo*, Rome, Carocci, 2006.

production itself creating a fundamental harmony between individual and collective interests. As always, the central imperative was to avoid division. The elimination of any kind of class conflict was of paramount importance because it was this that would permit the realization of the 'total' state. Arguments between theorists about precisely how the corporations should relate to the state continued during the 1930s, but no theorist denied this central principle of 'totality', to be produced by a common collective devotion to the objectives of the fascist state.

As is evident, this concept of the organic state—elaborated by Giovanni Gentile in his attempts to provide a coherent theory of Fascism—altered fundamentally the position of the individual within society. Any idea of a 'contract' between state and citizens was rejected. If the First World War had seen people demand increasingly that duties and sacrifices should be compensated by individual rights in respect of the state—in other words that people should be seen as participating citizens rather than as passive subjects—fascist ideology acknowledged any such rights only insofar as they were conducive to the workings of the state. Political rights were excluded, therefore, because, in the eyes of the fascists, any such rights could only be used to obstruct these workings and destroy national harmony. Essentially, under the fascist state, rights were concessions made by the state, in function of the state, and had no autonomous justification in citizenship. As concessions they could, of course, be withdrawn at the discretion of the state.[9] Such social improvements as were made during the fascist period were not made as a result of public pressure, therefore, but were 'handed down' from above, usually with the ultimate aim of strengthening the state. The expansion of the state maternity clinics

9. The question of duties (in this case military service) procuring rights (for the demobilized soldiers) arose in 1923. Fascist revision of the pension 'rights' of such soldiers (and the disabled) made clear that pensions were 'a gracious concession' of the state and not a response to 'acquired rights' consequent on the sacrifices of the soldiers. It is to be noted that pensions could be revoked for 'unbecoming behaviour', among which was, no doubt, the expression of any opposition to the regime. Cf. F. Quargliaroli, *Risarcire la nazione in armi*, Milan, Unicopli, 2018, ch. 5.

(ONMI) was a case in point: the birth of healthy babies represented excellent propaganda for the regime, but it was also encouraged because such babies would eventually make good soldiers. Eight million bayonets (Mussolini's vaunted objective) required eight million soldiers to hold them.

Pietro Costa has summed up well the relationship between individuals and rights under the regime, reflecting what has often been called the primacy of politics: 'A distinctive feature of Fascism is that it expressed with clarity the purely functional character of rights... subordinated to the superior interest of national power.'[10] Thus the door was opened to the political use of the law (as had been evident with the amnesty for crimes committed by the blackshirts, passed in December 1922, immediately after Mussolini's appointment as head of government) and the identification of the enemies of Fascism as enemies of the state, to be treated therefore as traitors.

Given the incessant references to the nation in fascist proclamations, an examination of provincial newspapers of the late 1930s might surprise the reader because of the attention given to social issues. There are frequent appeals for contributions to support this or that worthy cause—the fascist summer camps for the young, the local fascist youth movement, the poor and disabled, the maternity clinic, and so on. All couched in terms of what this paternal regime was doing for the people and all expressed in terms of national and social solidarity. In fact, fascist rhetoric made great use of the word 'solidarity' in respect of both local and national issues and talked a great deal about 'social justice'. Indeed the Labour Charter of 1927 went so far as to speak of the 'fundamental rights' of workers, always seen, of course, within the framework of the broader national interest. Italians—workers included—had to pull together for the greater good of the nation. The appeal to altruism, not unlike Hitler's programme of Winter Aid, was one of the many ways of attempting to engender

10. Costa, 'Lo Stato totalitario', p. 83.

a sense of community and could be supported for valid social reasons. However, this was a façade hiding the fact that it was a solidarity defined within the terms we have outlined above and prioritized, ultimately, not the well-being of the population but the strengthening of the state. In reality the much-vaunted (but little-demonstrated) social solidarity of the later 1930s spoke of the people but was really only interested in power. And, as already suggested, discipline, hierarchy, and obligation were the fundamental components of social organization, essential for the realization of the strong, compact, unified, fascist state.[11]

These were fascist priorities, the totalitarian ambitions; they were at the base of what was termed the 'fascist revolution'. On paper the project might look adventurous and even convincing, but what was essentially the utopian vision of theoreticians became much less credible when confronted with the realities of Italian society and the Italian economy. At that point—as we shall see—the project of the revolutionary construction of a new social and political system became little more than a hollow slogan; the revolution lost its way and outward show (the *esteriorità* much deprecated by many fascists) replaced substance. What did persist was the 'national' imperative which remained constant, justified repression, and continued to condition the fascist response to the problems the regime faced.

Hierarchies of benefit: wages, contracts, unions

Despite the repeated exaltation of the term, for many the idea of the ethical state was no doubt rather abstract. Much less abstract was the pay packet. For, if an exasperated nationalism motivated many fascists, many others—employers in particular—were motivated by other interests. As we have already seen, in many areas of northern and central Italy the violence of the blackshirts effectively broke the back of

11. M. S. Quine, *Italy's Social Revolution. Charity and Welfare from Liberalism to Fascism*, New York, Palgrave Macmillan, 2002, pp. 96–100.

the socialist organization and left workers and peasants with little or no defence against their employers, who had not supplied and financed the squads for purely altruistic or patriotic reasons. In rural areas an immediate effect of socialist defeat was a reduction in wages for labourers (accompanied, often, by an increase in hours worked) and, for sharecroppers, a worsening of contractual conditions. Such was the extent of the change in conditions that even people favourable to the regime denounced these situations of 'agrarian slavery'.[12]

For industrial workers the worsening of conditions was slower and probably less marked. Skilled workers enjoyed some defence in that they might be sacked but could not then be replaced as easily as could rural workers, who suffered the consequences of overpopulation. Even so, the defeat of the Occupation of the Factories left industrial workers very much on a back foot and, if the blackshirts rarely entered the factories because employers defended their own rights to exclusive control, a threatening fascist presence could still be felt outside the factory. In a process that lasted through much of the 1920s the industrial working class was reorganized around new methods of production—these were the years of Bedeaux and piecework—which saw the 'despecialization' of a large number of workers and the establishment of a new hierarchy within the factory. A small minority of workers gained from this reorganization; the vast majority lost. Wages were reduced; hours of work increased. Unlike their British and French counterparts, Italian workers had few defences. Protest became much more difficult, not only because non-fascist unions were first weakened and then abolished, but because the same process of reorganization had served to fragment worker solidarity, with any action having to be based on a single category, which would not then represent the collective action of a whole workforce.[13]

12. D'Annunzio's definition of agrarian Fascism. See Renzo De Felice, *Mussolini il fascista. I. La conquista del potere 1921–1925*, Turin, Einaudi, 1966, pp. 218, 257 note.
13. For industrial reorganization, see D. Bigazzi, *Il Portello. Operai, tecnici e imprenditori alla Alfa Romeo 1906–26*, Milan, Feltrinelli, 1988; G. Sapelli, *Fascismo, grande industria e sindacato. Il caso di Torino 1925–35*, Milan, Feltrinelli, 1975.

The fascist unions, given a monopoly in the representation of workers in 1926, rarely made up for the destruction of the socialist and Catholic unions. Although Edmondo Rossoni, a former revolutionary syndicalist, would attempt to gain some level of autonomy for the fascist unions, the corporative aim of reconciling the interests of bosses and workers was unrealistic, given the power relations that existed under the regime. Nonetheless, on occasions, the unions did make efforts to appear to work on behalf of the workers and sometimes the bosses would make small—usually not costly—concessions in order to bolster the control of the unions over the workforce. But the fascist unions generally lacked credibility, for obvious reasons, and accusations of collusion between employers and union leaders were common. By the end of the 1930s workers were complaining that the whole syndicalist structure was no more than a façade behind which their employers did very much as they liked. The corporations, which never really functioned, did nothing to reassure the workers or to protect their interests.[14]

At this point it is perhaps worth noting a significant difference from Nazism. Hitler was elected in 1933 at least in part because he promised to get millions of unemployed people back into work. For many, Nazism was seen as a promise of work—and wages. For all its obnoxious aspects, Nazism expressed an approach in respect of employment which was reflected in subsequent developments, when the Nazis did make efforts to listen to the demands of the working class and to respond to them—probably with some success.[15] On the contrary, almost the first impulse of Italian Fascism was to reduce wages and repress any form of worker protest. As a prominent fascist had put it, critically, in December 1920, the agrarian Fascism of the blackshirts was to be deplored because it was a 'white reaction' of the propertied

14. F. Cordova, *Il consenso imperfetto*, Soveria Mannelli, Rubbettino, 2010.
15. Of course, Hitler was not immediately successful in achieving continuing full employment. The economic difficulties of 1934, linked principally to problems of foreign exchange, saw widespread unemployment accompanied by popular disillusionment and discontent. See A. Tooze, *The Wages of Destruction. The Making and Breaking of the Nazi Economy*, New York, Viking, 2006, pp. 96–8.

classes (seeing the immediate success of this reaction, he soon changed his tune and praised it).[16] This fascist onslaught would be remembered by its victims; the, inevitable, hostility of workers and agricultural labourers to the fascist attack would remain throughout the twenty years of fascist rule, making ideological penetration far more difficult than it was to be in Nazi Germany. In 1939, when the Duce visited the Fiat factory in Turin, the workers crossed their arms and refused to applaud, forcing a furious Mussolini to leave the stage in silence.

Not everyone suffered under Fascism, of course. One of the features of the interwar years which most colours popular memory is the vast expansion of the urban lower middle class, created by the twin impulses of industrialization and urbanization. As fascist bureaucracy extended its range of activities on a national level through a multiplication of party and state bureaucratic organizations, the number of people employed in relatively stable jobs increased enormously. Many of them were women and all to some extent were dependent on the party and the regime for their continuing employment. This was a new social category—the public administration—which, together with a much more restricted professional and (to some extent) intellectual middle class, provided the backbone of fascist support. If for no other reason, economic interest suggested that they should defend their positions of relative advantage; a corporate spirit prevailed. While in no sense wealthy—the employees of government offices were those who dreamt of 'a thousand lire a month'[17]—this new class constituted a social category susceptible to the seductions of the regime on which they depended, even if, far from being revolutionary fascists, they were, in fact, a very conservative social group.[18]

We shall attempt in a moment to quantify the extent to which working conditions worsened for some as a consequence of the

16. Umberto Pasella, in P. Corner, *Fascism in Ferrara 1915–1925*, London, Oxford University Press, 1975, p. 129.
17. 'Se avessi mille lire al mese' ('If I had a thousand lira a month') is the title of a popular song of the time.
18. Mariuccia Salvati, *L'inutile salotto. L'abitazione piccolo-borghese nell'Italia fascista*, Turin, Bollati Boringhieri, 1993; but see also Salvati, 'The long history of corporativism'.

advent of Fascism, but here it is important to stress something that seems increasingly to have been lost to our memory of the regime but which should be glaringly obvious from what we have said so far. That is that Fascism was a class regime. To say this is not to revive some orthodox Marxist viewpoint, which sees Fascism exclusively as the expression of monopoly capitalism, nor is it to deny that fascist totalitarian theorists saw the movement as a revolutionary experiment that would resolve and go beyond class interests; it is simply to say that, in practice and very demonstrably, in its effects on the daily lives of many people, Fascism was a class regime in that it defended certain groups at the expense of others. This was nowhere more obvious than in the economic sphere. Under Fascism, on a simple scale of winners and losers in economic terms, we can see very clearly that those who lost were principally the industrial workers, dependent peasants, and landless agricultural labourers, while those who won—at least for a time—were mainly the middle and lower middle classes, including, in particular, state employees, together with those representing powerful industrial and agrarian interests, who increasingly occupied positions of command within the structure of the regime. Concentration on the figure of Mussolini obscures this fascist hierarchy of benefit. In reality fascist 'social solidarity' was based on a clear allocation of benefit, formally in the interests of the nation, in fact in the interests of certain social classes. In this class-based context, the idea that the corporations would function in the pursuit of some allegedly 'collective' harmony was, of course, an illusion that only the most determined believers in the fascist future could entertain.

Statistics rarely convince, but a few numbers may help to explode the myth that, under Fascism, 'we lived well'. The effect of the fascist conquest of power at the local level, even before the March on Rome, can be seen in the fact that between July 1921 and October 1922 real wages in industry fell by 21%.[19] Even making allowances for the fact

19. V. Zamagni, 'Una ricostruzione dell'andamento mensile dei salari industriali', in *Ricerche per la storia della Banca d'Italia*, vol. 5, Rome-Bari, Laterza, 1994, pp. 363, 367, 369; cit. in P. L. Ciocca, *Ricchi per sempre? Una storia economica d'Italia*, Turin, Bollati Boringhieri, 2007, p. 200.

that the international economy suffered a prolonged crisis after the crash of 1929, the decline in living conditions in Italy was, for many, far more marked than in other European countries. Following the revaluation of the lira in 1926/7 and the establishment of the absurdly high rate of exchange represented by Quota 90,[20] in 1927 wages were twice cut across the board by decree. Further reductions were decreed in 1930 and in 1934. It is true that prices also fell, but all calculations make it clear that wages fell much further, and much faster, than prices. Across the board wage increases after 1936 failed to compensate for rising prices and for increased deductions from pay packets. By 1938 industrial workers were earning, in real terms, 20% less than they had earned at the beginning of 1923—and they were working longer hours.[21] Conditions appear to have been particularly bad in the second half of the 1930s. A police informer reported from Milan in December 1936 that 'In many families, not only those of manual labourers but also in those of the middle and lower bourgeoisie, among state employees, professional people, and unemployed artisans, there is the blackest misery. Unfortunately people can't see any way out. On the contrary they are certain that things will get worse.'[22]

In the agricultural sector the situation was no better, with drastic cuts in wages, disregard for contracts, and no stability of employment. Many labourers were reduced to subsistence levels. Figures printed by the fascist union of Rovigo, for instance, show that, in 1931, labourers were earning only 60% of what they had been paid in 1921 (and this, given the source, was almost certainly an overestimation).[23]

20. The lira was anchored to the pound sterling at 90 lire to the pound; previous to revaluation it had been around 140 to the pound. For the effects, see Chapter 6.
21. See P. Corner, 'L'economia italiana fra le due guerre', in G. Sabattucci and V. Vidotto (eds), Storia d'Italia, vol. 4, Guerre e Fascismo, Rome-Bari, Laterza, 1997.
22. Quoted in A. De Bernardi [on Capoferri], in M. L. Betri, A. De Bernardi, I. Granata, and N. Torcellan, Il Fascismo in Lombardia. Politica, economia, e società, Milan, Franco Angeli, 1989.
23. On agricultural wages, see the still valid work of C. T. Schmidt, The Plough and the Sword, New York, Columbia University Press, 1938, ch. 8. More recent, on wages in general, see Zamagni, 'Una ricostruzione dell'andamento dei salari'; and on wages in industry, see G. Favero, 'Le statistiche dei salari industriali in periodo fascista', Quaderni storici, 2, 2010, pp. 319–57.

As is obvious, they had no redress. Protest on the part of day labourers meant simply that they did not find work again, and, in many cases, their houses, linked to their employment, might be put at risk. It is worth noting that, while Italian wage levels had risen continuously during the decade before the First World War, international comparisons show that Italy was the only European country with a consistently descending level of wages for the period 1920–39.

Private consumption was lower in the 1930s than it had been in the 1920s. A report published by the International Labour Organization (ILO) in Geneva in 1936 spelled out what this reduction signified when translated into figures for individual products. The striking feature—fully in line with the description of Fascism as a class regime—is that the difference between the working and middle classes increased markedly during the course of the regime. The ILO found that the families of dependent labour in agriculture ate half the quantities of meat, eggs, and dairy products consumed by urban lower middle and middle class families. Even more striking is the fact that, again according to the ILO, the population as a whole, surveyed in the period 1928–34, ate much less meat, eggs, butter, and very much less sugar, than the population in any other western European country (Spain and Portugal were not included). Rural workers were eating half as much again, therefore—often practically nothing.[24] These figures are confirmed by the historical records of the Italian Institute of Statistics (ISTAT), which show that calories consumed per head of the population were, on average, lower in the 1930s than in the previous decade.[25] Despite the Battle for Wheat (in reality, because of it, because it increased the cost of bread) people were eating fewer wheat-based products at the end of the 1930s than at the beginning of the 1920s.[26] In fact, such local studies as have been possible show that the families of labourers

24. International Labour Office, *Workers' Nutrition and Social Policy*, Geneva, 1936, pp. 208–33.
25. ISTAT, *Sommario di statistiche storiche italiane 1861–1955*, Rome, Istituto Poligrafico dello Stato, 1958, table 121.
26. G. Tattara, 'Cerealicoltura e politica agraria durante il Fascismo', in G. Toniolo (ed.), *Lo sviluppo economico italiano 1861–1940*, Rome-Bari, Laterza, 1973, p. 404.

consumed far fewer calories than required for hard physical labour, with the men getting by in the summer months, when employed most of the time, only because in that period they were given some meals by their employers. Indeed, in some regions of Italy, it seems surprising that people survived at all. As an appalled northern visitor to one of those poorer areas of the South wrote in 1928, 'misery is sovereign, impossible to find bread'.[27] Ten years later, an anonymous graffito on a wall in Rome would repeat the sentiment, referring to the large letter M to be seen everywhere on walls and buildings: 'M [ussolini] stands for misery'.

By 1939 living conditions in the towns had become very difficult. Here the regime was hoisted with its own petard. Claiming responsibility for everything that happened, it was considered responsible for what did not work. Shortages of coffee provoked serious popular criticism—a criticism that erupted into a more general protest against the regime. One informer's report provided a decalogue of popular grievances: 'They [the people] say that before Fascism this didn't happen, that there was coffee, that the bread was made of wheat, that the milk was genuine, that cloth was made of wool, that you could find everything, that pay was proportionate to the cost of living, that you didn't know what deductions were, that taxes were bearable, that commerce was stable, that work could be found, that people were happier, that you could express your own opinion...'[28] This was hardly a report on well-being. It is, however, interesting to note the way in which poor material conditions at this stage provoked hostile political comment.

Certainly Italy was still a relatively poor country, but these conditions were not created by any kind of 'absolute poverty' before which government was helpless. It is worth repeating that they were conditions determined by policies designed precisely to favour certain

27. Zannotti Bianchi quoted in P. Bevilacqua, *Le campagne del Mezzogiorno tra Fascismo e dopoguerra. Il caso della Calabria,* Turin, Einaudi, 1980, p. 90.
28. P. Corner, *The Fascist Party and Popular Opinion in Mussolini's Italy,* Oxford, Oxford University Press, 2012, p. 236.

groups, to ensure continued support for the regime, and—at least until 1929, when the international crisis changed the situation—to reassure foreign investors. All these objectives required the disciplining of labour and a reduction in the cost of labour. As Pier Luigi Ciocca, a former deputy director of the Bank of Italy, has written, 'the fascist movement, the violence, the Party, all corresponded to the basic needs of Italian capitalism to defend profits, to reaffirm permanently rights of property, and to re-establish command in the farms and in the factories'.[29] In this respect, in historical terms, there was little that was new. A poor standard of living and harsh conditions of work consti- tuted a part of what had always been 'the Italian road to accumulation' of capital, based on repression of the workforce rather than on its integration, and based on low levels of private consumption rather than an expansion of the internal market. These had been the central features of the process of rapid industrialization after 1860. What was new was that this repression was now built into the system of govern- ment and sanctified by government decree.

The social state: pensions, social insurance, assistance

'Wages may have gone down, but pensions compensated. And pen- sions, as everyone knows, were introduced by Mussolini.' This is still one of the most persistent canards in respect of the regime. Persistent, at least in part, because it is at the centre of the neo-fascist attempt to attribute to Fascism—and to the *Repubblica sociale* in particular—an enlightened social policy. It is enough to visit any of the websites of the neo-fascists to see that they are seeking a new legitimacy on the basis of policies proposed, but never realized, in the years between 1943 and 1945. Such websites rarely fail to mention that pensions had already been 'introduced' during the fascist regime.

29. Ciocca, *Ricchi per sempre?*, p. 192.

Of course, there were pensions paid during the regime and the system of social security was enhanced and reorganized, particularly with the creation of the INFPS in 1933.[30] But, as any serious study shows, the system of pensions and social insurance was devised and implemented in its fundamental structure before Mussolini came into power.[31] Following the German Bismarckian example, pensions were introduced by prime minister Francesco Crispi for certain, very limited, categories of employee (some public sector workers and army officers) in 1895 and this system, initially instituted on a voluntary basis, was progressively refined in the years before the First World War. With the war, the obligation of the state in respect of the families of soldiers at the front, the wounded and disabled, and the orphans, became obvious and the need for a much more extensive and inclusive insurance scheme was recognized by government—a realization reflected in the reforms of 1919 put through by prime ministers Orlando and Nitti. Social insurance became obligatory for many categories of worker, with employers' and workers' contributions going to fund unemployment subsidies, cover for accidents at work, and pensions. Benefits envisaged were often minimal, and favoured male rather than female workers. Even so, recognition of the state's responsibility for organizing social insurance represented a major precedent, ratified by the institution in 1919 of the Cassa Nazionale per le Assicurazioni Sociali.[32] Attempts were made to include even agricultural workers in the new scheme (a difficult category to insure because of the uncertain and seasonal nature of employment), but, in late 1923, during the first Mussolini government, these attempts were abandoned as a consequence of pressure from the agrarian bloc. The important feature of the post-war reforms was that they recognized compulsory social insurance as an essential feature of the modern

30. Istituto Nazionale Fascista di Previdenza Sociale—the state organization responsible for welfare policies, pensions, social insurance.
31. F. Conti and G. Silei, *Breve storia dello Stato sociale*, Rome, Carocci, 2013.
32. On these developments, see Giovanna Procacci, *Warfare-welfare. Intervento dello Stato e diritti dei cittadini (1914–18)*, Rome, Carocci, 2013, pp. 45–95.

state; provision for unemployment and for pensions was seen to be a duty of the state and a necessity for a stable society, giving a large number of workers (perhaps some 40% of the workforce) established rights. All this, *before* the advent of Fascism.

The fascist regime inherited this system, and, during the *ventennio*, modified and extended it, often in a very piecemeal fashion. At the same time the regime introduced important limitations on benefits, restricted categories of beneficiaries, and gradually reduced the state's contributions to the insurance fund. For example, share-croppers and tenant farmers were excluded by the reform of 1923 and disabled pensioners also saw their benefits reduced. Subsidies for involuntary unemployment had so many conditions attached that there was a strong disincentive to claim benefit. Many employers resisted paying their contributions and sanctions against non-payment were watered down and rarely put into effect.

As with many authoritarian regimes, social benefits were conceded at the same time as political rights were denied. The fascist impulse was essentially that of the centralization of initiatives, reducing the role previously played by local elites and by charitable institutions in relieving poverty. Centralization was intended to increase efficiency but it also permitted the regime to emphasize the fact that assistance sprang from the concession of the fascist state and not from private institutions, nor from any imagined rights of citizens. With the constitution of the INFPS, social insurance—covering not only pensions but also illness and unemployment benefits—became one of the pillars of the regime, to the extent that, by the end of the decade, following rapid and chaotic expansion, the INFPS was the second largest employer in Italy.[33] In this context it should be noted that workers'

33. For a detailed analysis of the evolution of INFPS, see Melis, *Macchina imperfetta*, pp. 448–67. For a general survey of social policy, see C. Giorgi and Ilaria Pavan, *Storia dello Stato sociale in Italia*, Bologna, Il Mulino, 2020, ch. 2, as well as C. Giorgi, *La previdenza del regime. Storia dell'Inps durante il Fascismo*. Bologna, Il Mulino, 2004 and, more recently, C. Giorgi, 'Le politiche sociali del Fascismo', *Studi storici* 1, 2014, pp. 93–107. Also useful is S. Inaudi, *A tutti indistintamente. L'Ente opera assistenziale nel periodo fascista*, Bologna, Clueb, 2008.

contributions to INFPS consistently greatly exceeded the benefits paid out and that the surplus represented an invaluable source of finance for the state in funding costly projects such as those regarding land reclamation, and providing much of the capital for the financing of the state holding company, IRI (and, thus, the refinancing of banks and industry), during the latter part of the 1930s. It was the reorganization of the system around the state and its great expansion that permitted the regime to boast that the fascist state was caring for its citizens and providing pensions *ex nova*. The paternalism of Fascism was evident here; indeed it was highlighted, in the sense that all social benefits received by the population were to be attributed to the generosity of Mussolini himself.

The myth of the 'fascist pension' derives from this propagandistic attribution. In reality, in the interwar years and following the experience of the First World War, social insurance for the population was being introduced by governments throughout Europe; it was part of the process of governments coming to terms with a new and very vocal mass society. In Italy the process coincided with Fascism and was directed by the regime, but it was in no sense an exclusive of Fascism nor was it an invention of a generous Duce. If anything, the system constructed by the regime arrived later than in many other European countries and provided less in terms of benefits.

That said, the way in which social insurance was organized and implemented by the regime bears many of the hallmarks of fascist priorities. Certainly, this was not the welfare state of Lord Beveridge. The system was in no way universal, extending to all individuals on the basis of citizenship; it was based on concession, not on social rights. And, as we have seen, it was a system that created dependence for its beneficiaries on the discretionary decisions of, at the local level, the PNF-dominated public administration.[34] Indeed, the most striking feature of the system developed during the 1920s and 1930s was

34. M. Ferrero, *Il welfare state in Italia. Sviluppo e crisi in prospettiva comparata*, Bologna, il Mulino, 1984.

its immense fragmentation, with every different category of worker
having its own pension structure. This permitted a myriad differences
in treatment based on hierarchy, and the fragmentation was used,
undoubtedly, to the advantage of those groups of workers considered
most favourable to the regime. Among these were the state employees
of the burgeoning machine of state bureaucracy—an arena in which
the accentuation of internal hierarchies through differentiation of
treatment permitted a very successful policy of *divide et impera* on the
part of the regime, with employees defending their privileges of
category against those below them, while aspiring to the privileges
of those in the category above them.[35]

The hierarchy of benefit, so often reflecting both class and gender
differences, with gender reinforcing distinctions made on the grounds
of class, is illustrated well by the amounts envisaged for marriage
grants and prizes for having children. On marriage, male white collar
employees (*impiegati*) received 1,000 lire, industrial waged workers
700, and agricultural labourers 500. The corresponding figures for
women were 700, 500, 400 lire. The same hierarchy of class was applied
to prizes for producing children, with the difference that, while white
collar and industrial workers received the same amount, agricultural
workers received only half the sums allocated to their fellow Italians.
Family allowances were conceded with the same preferences, all
rigidly linked to the position of the male 'breadwinner'.[36] Class pref-
erence was further evident in the fact that benefits for the children of
workers ceased when the child reached 16, while those for the children of white collar workers continued until 18. Conversely, when it
came to pensions, industrial workers paid a higher proportion of their
earnings (15–20%) to central funds than did white collars (10–12%),
yet pensions paid to the latter were more than double those paid to

35. Mariuccia Salvati, 'Lo stato sociale in Italia. Caratteri originali e motivi di una crisi',
    Passato e presente, 1994, p. 32. The implications of category fragmentation are con-
    firmed in Melis, *Macchina imperfetta*, pp. 111–18.
36. See Quine, *Social Revolution*, pp. 126–7.

the former.[37] Even within a regime of apparent paternal welfare, the social priorities of Fascism remained very evident.

As in many countries, the centralization of structures corresponded to an increasing element of state control of those economic issues that touched the ordinary citizen, compelling, undoubtedly, a greater integration of state and society. Under Fascism, this meant the establishment of a monopoly of distribution of benefit at the local level. As already noted, party and state bureaucratic organizations controlled almost everything bar the Church, with obvious consequences for the population. Even if not stated openly the message was 'anti-fascists need not apply'. If propaganda would inevitably give insurance provisions a very positive spin, it is clear that the extension of welfare had another, more repressive, face. Compulsory insurance became, therefore, one of the many mechanisms of social control. Need or entitlement might be recognized but political criteria could be the determinants in deciding how the offices would respond. In fact, statistics show, for example, that many unemployed who qualified for benefit did not make application, presumably anticipating refusal. The discretionary power of the fascist bureaucracy was again in evidence. Many of those with insurance entitlement would draw the obvious conclusion: it was better to conform than to contest.

Social insurance was, therefore, at one and the same time an aspect of modernization and a means of engendering discipline. Despite this latter aspect, no one should doubt that pensions, insurance against illness and unemployment, family allowances, and so on were useful in inducing favourable attitudes towards the regime. Because of the extent of state control, allocation of scarce resources is always one of the strong cards of dictatorship, particularly in poor countries, and Italy was no exception. As vehicles for creating consensus, INFPS and related agencies were probably very effective, therefore. For many

37. For figures, see U. Belloni, *La previdenza sociale a favore dei lavoratori*, Novara, PNF, 1940 and Istituto Nazionale Fascista per la Previdenza Sociale (INFPS), *Al di là del lavoro e al di là del salario*, Rome, 1942.

Italians, the state as benefactor was an entirely novel experience—one that could not pass unnoticed. Particularly during the years of acute economic crisis, assistance provided by the regime was likely to produce recognition on the part of those who received it, even if that assistance was always heavily politicized.[38]

Domestic Fascism: family, health, and housing

If the issue of wages and pensions hardly reinforces the legend of 'we lived well', the health of the fascist nation is one of the areas in which the nostalgics and the neo-fascists would seem to stand on firmer ground. And with reason. After all, there was the battle against malaria, the battle against tuberculosis, there was the demographic campaign, there was ONMI[39] which helped young mothers and reduced significantly infant mortality, and then there were the holiday camps for the young. Sports and other leisure activities also flourished in the 1920s and 1930s and workers could relax and regain energy in the *dopolavoro* (the fascist after-work organization).[40] It all seems to add up to a picture of a strong and healthy society—in fact, exactly the picture fascist newsreels still show us, that of a formerly traditional and backward nation entering a new modernity in a dynamic and organized manner.

Certainly the modernizing thrust of the regime is very evident in this area and it would be unrealistic to deny beneficial effects for the population. But, as with social insurance, in the field of public health the regime boasted many 'realizations' and 'conquests' that depended little on original initiatives of the fascist movement. As many studies of social reform make clear, there is a surprising level of continuity

---

38. On Lombardy in the crisis, see S. Colarizi, in M. L. Betri et al., *Fascismo in Lombardia*; also, for Turin during the crisis, Corner, *Fascist Party*, pp. 185–92.
39. Opera Nazionale Maternità Infanzia—the state organization responsible for the instruction of young mothers.
40. V. De Grazia, *The Culture of Consent. Mass Organisation of Leisure in Fascist Italy*, Cambridge, Cambridge University Press, 1981.

between the period before Fascism and the fascist period itself in the sense that many projects for social reform preceded the advent of Fascism and were subsequently fed into the policies of the regime.

In the decades before 1922 there had been an ongoing debate in much of Europe about questions relating to the quality of population, with topics such as race, eugenics, public hygiene, and social and environmental reform at its centre. Italian academics and scientists were heavily involved in these discussions. These, essentially biopolitical, debates took on a new urgency with the First World War when many countries became acutely aware of the fact that their soldiers had not been in good physical condition when recruited. Furthermore the enormous losses of men posed a fresh problem for the post-war period. As a consequence, even in the most belligerent countries politicians recognized that the state had both to replace its population losses and to improve the conditions of its survivors.

Mussolini assumed power with these objectives already clearly defined by his predecessors. In a sense he rode the wave of projected social reforms, designed to improve conditions in key areas and already on the political agenda. Again, it was a question of adapting government objectives to the needs of a newly politically conscious mass society and of finding people who could realize these objectives. In this last respect, the regime was in no way averse to the employment of specialists and technicians not linked to the fascist movement, and some highly competent social reformers welcomed the opportunity offered by the regime for the implementation of their ideas, turning a blind eye to the fact that the price paid for this opportunity was the repression of political liberties. The efforts of such people permitted the regime to restructure and reorganize many already existing initiatives in the field of public health, introduce some new ideas, and—fundamentally—to bring everything under the central control of the fascist state. Thus, for example, the clinic for mothercare that had existed in Pistoia since 1900 as a private, charitable structure run by local doctors was taken over in 1925 by the newly created fascist maternity agency and became a state-run clinic, while performing the same functions as before.[41] Here, as with many of the after-work leisure structures and even with certain of the camps for children, the name simply changed over the door. What was important, however, was that with that change they became fascist organizations and so invited people to associate their operation directly with the regime and with the state. As was obvious, as state-run organizations, it was often the local PNF which decided who was eligible for benefit.

To return to a theme already touched on, it is important to recognize that it was during the 1920s and 1930s that many people, particularly in rural areas, came into contact with a state that did not just collect taxes and repress protest but seemed to show some concern for its citizens. The contemporary memory of Fascism, if it is sometimes favourable in certain respects, undoubtedly owes a great deal to this apparent novel concern. However, in historical terms, we have to distinguish between what people thought the state was doing for them and the real objectives of the state. This is particularly true in respect of the question of demography.[42]

Demographic concerns were at the centre of much of fascist thinking. It was demography with a difference, however, because its fundamental aim was to increase the population in order to further the great power ambitions of the regime. So many of the policies relating to the health of the population were based on ideas that saw the individual in terms of his or her function for the state; thus individual well-being was not an objective in itself but only insofar as it contributed to the creation of a strong state. The pro-natalist policies followed by the regime, ranging, as we have seen, from maternity benefits to prizes for large families, and taxes on unmarried men were inspired by the conviction that there was—to put it briefly—strength in

41. P. Guarnieri, 'Dagli aiuti materni all'ONMI. L'assistenza alla maternità e all'infanzia del Fascismo', in L. Pozzi and M. Breschi (eds), *Salute, malattie, sopravvivenza in Italia fra '800 e '900*, Udine, Forum, 2007. Continuity only went so far, however. Doctors in the clinic, told to take the Party card, resigned their posts.

42. Quine, *Social Revolution*; C. Ipsen, *Dictating Demography. The Problem of Population in Fascist Italy*, Cambridge, Cambridge University Press, 1996.

numbers and that, unlike other European countries which were experiencing a decline in population (in part as a consequence of the war), Italy should pass from the thirty-six million of 1921 to sixty million by 1950. The reasoning opened the door to racial theories of Italian 'superiority', of course, because Italians were to show a strong capacity for reproduction and demonstrate the difference between Italy and the other European powers, judged by this measure to be 'old', 'weak', and excellent examples of Oswald Spengler's 'Decline of the West'.

The campaigns for the eradication of malaria and tuberculosis, in themselves enlightened, were pursued as a part of these objectives. They, like other 'battles' of the regime,[43] were excellent vehicles for popular mobilization and undoubtedly served in this respect, but few were left in doubt (indeed, the constant use of military language made it obvious) that ensuring a healthy population was part of a larger scheme of national affirmation and expansion. In the event, many of the programmes and projects were only partially successful, sometimes due to lack of funds, sometimes due to organizational and bureaucratic obstacles, and sometimes because they trod too heavily on the toes of established interests. The incidence of malaria was reduced (although, for its eradication, it would have to wait for American DDT after the Second World War) and there was some slight growth in population, more due to a reduction in infant mortality (which, however, remained high by European standards) than to an absolute increase in live births. Despite the new clinics, tuberculosis remained a scourge throughout the *ventennio*. Abortion, which was illegal and firmly discouraged by the regime because of the demographic campaign, seems to have remained high, although here figures are inevitably very unreliable.[44]

The regime made considerable efforts to encourage large families and sought to reinforce the paternal role within the family, defining

43. The demographic 'battle' was accompanied by the Battle for Wheat, the Battle for the Lira, the Zootechnical Battle, and so on.
44. Quine, *Social Revolution*, pp. 251–2 in particular but *passim*.

the female role increasingly in terms of maternity and the home.[45] However, in reality, as the statistics suggest, for many people there were few incentives to produce babies; prizes for large families could not outweigh other factors. The 1930s was a period of prolonged depression, something reflected in the fact that, despite the celibacy laws which taxed unmarried men, and the inducement of prizes, marriage rates continued to fall and—in part because people began to marry later—birth rates were lower than they had been in the decade before. Unless you worked for the state (and even then, many categories of office workers pleaded poverty), it was likely that pay was bad and uncertain and, as we have seen, food was poor (which no doubt accounts for the renewed incidence of pellagra during the 1930s).[46]

That said, in part because of the demographic priorities, in part because of factors that affected all European countries following the First World War, the position of women in Italian society certainly changed under the regime. While peasant women continued to bear a heavy workload, urbanization encouraged new patterns of behaviour for others. In the towns more women went out to work, which meant that, even if they were invariably paid less than men (often half the male salary), they escaped the claustrophobic family for a time.[47] As statistics show, female employment in the public sector increased significantly and the percentage of girls receiving secondary and university education continued to rise, if only gradually. More women became participants in social and political associations: just as the regime attempted to create 'New Men', so it also looked to the realization of 'New Women'. Thus the fascist movement created roles for women—sometimes very public roles—within the *fasci femminili* and the *massaie rurali* (rural housewives) organization, and units of women

45. See M. Salvante, *La paternità nell'Italia fascista. Simboli, esperienze e norme, 1922–1943*, Rome,Viella, 2020.
46. Pellagra increased by a factor of ten between 1932 and 1939. See D. Preti, *La modernizzazione corporativa (1920–40)*, Milan, Franco Angeli, 1987, pp. 64–65.
47. For accounts of the 'escape' from the family, see P. Willson, *The Clockwork Factory. Women and Work in Fascist Italy*, Oxford, Clarendon Press, 1993.

and girls were always present in official parades and in gymnastic exhibitions. In short, at least in theory, women became participants in the fascist national crusade and this did change the position of women in respect of the state, to which formally they—and not only the men—now had 'fascist' obligations.

Yet, while this development can be read as indicating a certain 'empowerment' of women within Italian society, too great an emphasis on this theme may hide the reality of the situation. Fascist insistence on the subordinate position of women within the family made clear that, whatever increased liberties women enjoyed outside the home, these were to be enjoyed within the context of male domination and without sacrificing the family. Despite important changes in roles, the regime aimed fundamentally at a 'gender restoration' after the chaos of the Great War and the patriarchal model was always stressed.[48] Mussolini was himself portrayed as the model of male prowess and the fascist movement, with its emphasis on conflict, war, and death, had always been, and was to remain, intensely *maschilista*. Employment policies (which attempted—largely unsuccessfully[49]—to defend male workers against the arrival of women in the factories) and family policies (which reinforced the role of the male breadwinner) did nothing more than reflect these priorities. Mussolini's well-known phrase that 'war is to men as motherhood is to women' said it all.

Housing was also a particularly acute problem. Many of the reports and inquiries filed during the 1930s speak of appalling housing in many areas, both in the North and in the South, with families living in one room with neither running water nor any other form of sanitation. Many shared the one room with animals. For instance, in 1936 the prefect of Pescara wrote of his city, 'If we were to look carefully at

---

48. See A. Pescarolo, *Il lavoro delle donne nell'Italia contemporanea*, Rome, Viella, 2019, ch. 8. In general, see V. De Grazia, *How Fascism Ruled Women. Italy 1922–45*, Berkeley, University of California Press, 1993.

49. In certain industries—for instance the textile industry—women were simply better workers. For employer preferences, see P. Corner, 'Donne, Fascismo, e mercato del lavoro', in P. Corner, *Riformismo e Fascismo*, Rome, Bulzoni, 2001, pp. 249–66.

criteria of hygiene and housing suitability the greater part of the
houses should be termed uninhabitable.' The difficulties in reducing
the incidence of TB and other illnesses were linked to these conditions. Indeed, in Pescara it was reported that, of the 572 cases of TB
reported between 1932 and 1936, almost all were related to families
who lived on the ground floor, of whom 425 had neither WC nor
running water, and 227 had no window. As doctors observed at the
time, it was pointless to construct clinics to treat people if the basic
conditions that engendered the disease remained unchanged.[50]

The fascist government was not responsible for these extreme conditions but it did little to improve the situation. Starting in 1925, there
had been a progressive relaxation in housing controls, probably with
the intention of releasing housing to the market and increasing levels
of private ownership. But, because of the shortage of housing, deregu-
lation produced a spiral in both house prices and rents which pushed
the poor into worse housing. And the regime failed in its efforts to
encourage the building of new houses. Apart from certain schemes
that aimed to build houses for state employees, social housing, already
a feature of the liberal era, developed little during the regime and, as
with so many other aspects of life under Fascism, the allocation of
benefit was at the discretion of the local fascist authorities.[51] It was a
common accusation that the first houses had been given to the needy
for propaganda purposes, the rest to the 'friends' of the PNF. In com-
parative terms Britain built six times as many houses in the 1930s as
did Italy; France and Germany built twice as many. Where new houses
were built it was often as a result of the destruction of ancient urban
centres for purposes of exhibition, as occurred in Rome with the *via
dell'Impero*, with the affected population pushed into crowded and

50. C. Felice, *Il disagio di vivere*, Milan, Franco Angeli, 1989, pp. 211–12; also Preti,
    Modernizzazione, p. 185.
51. According to Quine, more than half of the 52,000 flats built up to 1935 were designated
    specifically for employees in the public administration. Quine, *Social Revolution*, p. 122.

badly planned suburbs where their conditions remained almost equally unsatisfactory.[52]

Justice, legality—and the mafia

The myth of the 'firm hand' of the dictator when it comes to dealing with criminality still has its appeal for some. Even today, the idea that there was justice under Fascism remains strong. According to popular legend, the fascist regime first restored and then guaranteed order, authority made itself felt, crime received its due reward, and—of course—Mussolini eliminated the mafia. It is a narrative that makes authoritarian government attractive to some Italians today, precisely because of their irritation over the perceived weakness of the democratic state, with its laws passed to benefit individuals, its absurdly lengthy trials, and its prescriptions—aspects of what is considered to be a corrupt political class and a lethargic judicial system that all too frequently appears to let the guilty go free.

Few of the legends regarding Fascism are more misguided than this, however—and no convinced fascist would have sought to justify the movement in terms of respect for the laws of liberal Italy. A regime that was founded on the exercise of illegal violence could hardly present itself as being a serious supporter of conventional legality. To justify their actions fascist blackshirts did not make reference to the existing law—the Zanardelli legal code of 1892—but to what they termed a 'higher law'—that of the Nation as they conceived it. According to this conception, as we have seen, killing socialists was an act of 'purification' of a contaminated nation and reflected obedience to the moral imperatives of a new kind of state. The same justification for a 'higher law' was given by Mussolini when, on 3 January 1925, he effectively admitted responsibility for the murder of socialist deputy,

52. See B. P. F. Wanrooj, 'Italian society under Fascism', in A. Lyttelton (ed.), *Liberal and Fascist Italy*, Oxford, Oxford University Press, 2002.

Matteotti. That such a 'higher law' patently did not exist was no obstacle to its invocation; it appeared to give legitimacy to actions that existing legal codes could never do. Moreover it seemed to many fascists to be a guarantee of impunity in the law courts.

This dual concept of legality—ordinary law and fascist 'law'—was partly resolved with the establishment of the regime in 1925 and the passage of the repressive 'most fascist' laws between 1925 and 1926 which permitted formal legal proceedings against individuals and activities previously dealt with in summary fashion by the squads. Effectively, because these laws reproduced much of the highly repressive legislation of the First World War, 'normal' life became that of a permanent state of emergency.[53] Active anti-Fascism became a crime against the Nation; anti-fascists became non-Italians and their property could be confiscated. After 1926 what were considered the more serious anti-fascist crimes, in particular acts performed or projected against the figure of the Duce, were tried by the newly created Special Tribunal for the Defence of the State. Even so, and even with the revision of the penal codes with the Rocco Legal Code (1930) which further defined anti-fascist activities, fascist violence remained common and was rarely prosecuted. Where fascists were prosecuted, they received short sentences or were acquitted—often by magistrates who followed carefully the administrative directives coming from the Ministry and knew what was good for their future career.[54] In short, anti-Fascism was a crime, tantamount to treason, whereas the violence of overactive fascist thugs was to be accepted and overlooked because it was conceived to be 'pedagogical' in nature and therefore, ultimately, in the interests of the state itself.

53. On the continuities in the repressive use of the concept of 'state of emergency', see Procacci, *Warfare-welfare*.
54. The judiciary seems to have offered little resistance to political pressures. See G. Focardi, *Magistratura e Fascismo. L'amministrazione della giustizia in Veneto 1920–1945*, Venice, Marsilio, 2012, and M. Sbriccoli, 'Le mani nella pasta e gli occhi al cielo. La penalistica italiana negli anni del Fascismo', *Quaderni fiorentini*, 28, 1999 pp. 817–50. Sbriccoli underlines the degree to which the legislation of liberal Italy had strong repressive tendencies which the regime was able to exploit.

The Italian politician and lawyer Piero Calamandrei wrote of the 'duality' of fascist legality, noting that there was a façade of respect for the legal codes but, in practice, a 'falsification' of the law because of favouritism, political pressure, and corruption, producing what was, in effect, a regime of illegality.[55] In respect of legal procedures, it should be remembered that alleged miscreants were often brought to trial as a result of the operation of police spies working for the Polizia Politica or for the OVRA. While casual, day-to-day, expressions of hostility to the regime were often punished with an extrajudicial beating in the local fascist headquarters, the more serious political opposition was dealt with much more systematically and, as Franzinelli has documented, with methods that resemble those of many other dictatorial regimes.[56] This aspect of the regime should not be underestimated. Fascist Italy was not the kind of police state Orwell has described but it had many aspects in common with such a state. It was a world that exploited fear—fear of the uncertain and discretionary nature of fascist 'justice'. It was a world in which denunciations were encouraged, informers widely used, traps laid, confessions extorted (sometimes by torture), prisoners 'turned' by blackmail, betrayals rewarded. Hotel porters, doormen in blocks of flats, taxi drivers, street cleaners—these were all urged to keep their eyes and ears open and report if necessary. Failing to report a 'seditious' comment overheard in the train or tram could land a listener in trouble; it was an offence, and sometimes a listener would ask others to moderate their comments because of fear of the consequences. By the end of the 1930s fear of denunciation seems to have been widespread, provoking—as we have seen—a wariness of unguarded expression which was all that was needed to discourage people from talking.

The *Tribunale speciale* was an aspect of this. It was, in effect, a kind of kangaroo court—a court fit for the purpose of working, not on the

---

55. Quoted in Costa, 'Lo stato totalitario', p. 97.
56. M. Franzinelli, *I tentacoli dell'OVRA. Agenti, collaboratori e vittimi cella polizia politica fascista*, Turin, Bollati Boringhieri, 1999, chs 4, 7, 9.

basis of the civil code, but rather on that of the military code—and the severe wartime military code at that. The accused could not choose a lawyer; he or she had to be content with a defence lawyer appointed by the court itself. In defiance of the principles of Cesare Beccaria, the death penalty was restored for crimes judged to be 'political' in nature and there was no right of appeal against these sentences. Although only a few death sentences were handed down in the course of the court's existence (thirty-one, with public execution by militiamen of the MVSN), the *Tribunale* sentenced many (5,620 for the record) to long periods of imprisonment and more than 12,000 to the internal exile of *confino*. It was on the one hand a showcase of fascist 'justice', intended to demonstrate fascist rigour to the general public; on the other it represented an arena in which police could more or less act as they wished, with a flexibility and a discretionary power not available through the actions of the ordinary courts. If more anti-fascists did not appear before the court it was because many were sent to *confino* by administrative order of the prefect of the province where they had been arrested, thus not facing trial.[57]

Some—relatively few—anti-fascists may have escaped trial because they were committed directly to psychiatric institutions. Committal was based on a simple administrative order from the provincial authorities and there was no possibility of appeal. Many so interned had not committed any offence; but open and repeated declarations of opposition to the regime could be classified as clear evidence of mental illness. The reasoning was that if you were against Mussolini you were obviously mad. Indefinite detention was thus permitted on the basis of threat to public order.[58] As is well known but all too often

57. M. Franzinelli, *Il tribunale del Duce. La giustizia fascista e le sue vittime (1926–43)*, Milan, Mondadori, 2017. Compared with Nazi Germany, the Soviet Union, or Franco's Spain, the number of political executions is, of course, low—something that has contributed to the view of Fascism as representing a 'lesser evil'. As this book attempts to argue, it is more the system of repression than the numbers that is the central issue.

58. P. Giovannini, 'Esclusione, abandono, e morte. Gli ospedali psichiatrici in Italia', *Storia e problemi contemporanei*, 24, 2011; M. Petracci, *I matti di Mussolini. Manicomi e repressione politica nell'Italia fascista*, Rome, Donzelli, 2014.

forgotten, Ida Dalser, Mussolini's partner of 1914, and their son, Benito Albino, were consigned to mental institutions during the regime because the embarrassment they caused the fascist leader, now married to Donna Rachele, was judged to justify permanent detention. Both died in confinement.[59]

There is nothing in prison statistics to indicate one of the great legends relating to Fascism—that fascist rigour was successful in reducing crime—has any basis in fact. The numbers incarcerated remain fairly constant through the interwar years, with no evidence of decline. Nor is there any significant change in the number of crimes committed, the only exception being a rise in persons sentenced for theft in the second half of the 1930s—presumably an indication of worsening economic conditions for a part of the population.

Some crimes rarely appear in the statistics, of course, because they can be difficult to chart. One of these is corruption. There are good reasons for thinking that corruption reached new levels under Fascism, although it is not easy to arrive at the evidence—because the corrupt were the fascists themselves. In this the fascist dictatorship was no different from many other dictatorships. The increase in corruption depended on a number of factors. The lack of independent controls on behaviour, a tame press, a persistent sense of impunity before the law, the knowledge that the Party preferred to turn a blind eye rather than risk a scandal—all contributed to a situation in which many fascists, particularly at the local level, felt that they could do more or less as they liked, ignoring the law and enjoying the spoils of their victory. Reports reaching Rome testified to the fact that some provincial officials were making money on a grand scale through a variety of means, most of which amounted to barefaced extortion. 'Voluntary contributions' to Party funds were often far from voluntary and often found a different destination. It was a very open exploitation of public office

---

59. See L. Benadusi (ed.), *'Mussolini ha deciso di internarmi col piccino'. Lettere di Ida Dalser a Luigi Albertini 1916–1925*, Milan, Fondazione Corriere della sera, 2010, Introduzione. It remains unclear whether Mussolini and Dalser were formally married or not, partly because of the subsequent tampering with the official records.

and public authority for private gain—ironic for a movement which proposed that private, individual interests should disappear in the interests of the national community. Instead, as we have already observed, what was public often became private.[60] Family, friends, and locality frequently had priority over the Nation.[61] Evidently the rhetoric about collective, 'totalitarian' solidarity so often pedalled by theorists of the fascist state did not govern everyone's behaviour.

Mussolini, not himself involved in any corrupt practices as far as we know, was undoubtedly well aware of what certain of his more important supporters were doing—it was known to everyone. It was impossible not to see what the Ciano family was up to, or even, for that matter, to ignore the benefits accruing to the family of Mussolini's mistress, Claretta Petacci. But the Duce preferred to do nothing about it. Apart from the issue of probable scandal, the fascist leader understood that, in a regime that rested heavily on a whole network of personal contacts, corruption represented a kind of glue, keeping the network together. Besides, in some cases, as with Farinacci[62] and his grossly inflated lawyer's fees, it was always useful to have some compromising information on his followers to produce if they ever became difficult. Mussolini was very adept at hinting to his subordinates that he knew more about their activities than they would have liked.

Then, finally, where justice and the law is concerned, there is the question of the mafia. One of the great legends related to the regime is that Mussolini eradicated the Sicilian mafia. This was certainly one of the principal propaganda planks of the fascist government; the message was that the regime acted decisively and looked no one in the face. Cesare Mori, the 'iron prefect', became, for a time, almost a national hero because of his extremely harsh operations in Sicily—

60. On the general problem of corruption, see P. Corner, 'Corruzione di sistema? I "fascisti reali" tra pubblico e privato', in M. Palla and P. Giovannini (eds), *Il fascismo dalle mani sporche. Dittatura, corruzione, affarismo*, Rome-Bari, Laterza, 2019.
61. On this theme, see R. J. B. Bosworth, 'Everyday Mussolinismo. Friends, family, locality, and violence in Fascist Italy', *Contemporary European History*, 14, 2005.
62. Roberto Farinacci, radical fascist leader from Cremona; identified by Hitler as a possible successor to Mussolini.

hundreds of arrests, deportations, violent attacks on villages considered to be dominated by the various mafia groups. Certainly this was action, and on a large scale. But was it successful? The answer is complex. As Salvatore Lupo has shown, the regime wished to weaken any alternative centres of authority or control and the mafia was just such a separate centre of authority within Sicily. Just as Catholic youth organizations were always contested by the regime, so the mafia represented a challenge to totalitarian pretensions. But the campaign against the mafia also related to the power relations within Sicily. Intransigent Sicilian fascists presented themselves as the representatives of the new against the old. They hoped to use the fascist movement in order to destroy the control of a mafia-centred traditional elite—an elite that had retained its connection with liberal politicians rather than passing wholeheartedly to the regime. Mori's campaign was aimed principally at certain elements of this traditional group, and he was effective in this respect, making hundreds of arrests and staging maxi-trials in which large numbers of accused were sentenced. At the same time, however, he also moved against the supposedly 'new' men of the intransigent fascists, guilty of creating their own power base, once again independent of the control of Rome. In this last campaign he was only partially successful. The upshot was that the large landed proprietors, who, in the final analysis, remained the principal referents of the regime, remained untouched, but they now made more reference directly to Rome and less to the mafia.

Mori was 'retired' in 1929, more or less forcibly, and those who followed him showed less determination in their actions. Faced with a resurgence of rural mafia in the mid-1930s, a new campaign against the mafia was waged (in great silence because, officially, Mori had already dealt with the problem) but with relatively little effect. What is clear is that, in 1943 when the Anglo-Americans landed in Sicily, the mafia was still there, ready to emerge more strongly in the new political conditions of the post-war.[63]

63. See S. Lupo,'L'utopia totalitaria del Fascismo 1918–1942', in M. Aymard and G. Giarrizzo (eds), *Storia dell'Italia. Le regioni dall'Unità ad oggi. La Sicilia*, Turin, Einaudi, 1997.

This alone is sufficient to suggest that those equations of the fascist nostalgics—dictatorship means elimination of the mafia, democracy means rebirth of the mafia—are oversimplified. Rather, what the story does make clear is the difficulties the regime faced when dealing with a society split into contesting factions, where energetic action against one of the factions simply opened a door to another, and where the imperative of enforcing order had to be balanced with that of maintaining support for the regime. As with so many other aspects of the regime, the fascist government found that, in order to affirm its hold, it had to compromise with local power, in one guise or another, and, in Sicily, all too often that local power was contaminated with mafia.

5

Mussolini

Twentieth-century statesman?

It is difficult—perhaps impossible—to think of a dictator who did not want to cut a figure on the international scene. Given that an accentuated nationalism is invariably a large component of the dictatorial message, this is hardly surprising. International recognition is, after all, a measure of success for a politician and an extremely potent weapon to be used with the population at home. One can be sure that Nicolai Ceauşescu's audience with Queen Elizabeth II in 1978 was not allowed to go unnoticed in Bucharest or Timişoara. And, indeed, it remains an encounter difficult to forget, largely because of its implications for international relations. In a sense, the event was greater than the man. In the same way, the international events surrounding dictators often seem to give them a standing that a straightforward assessment of their internal politics might deny them. In the case of Mussolini this is certainly so. Many are disposed to argue that, whatever his faults, which are not denied, he put Italy on the map. In a country permanently convinced that it is not given the credit it is due, this argument has some force; even among his critics there is the sneaking suspicion that at least Mussolini made Italy count. In some circles, he remains surrounded by the aura of the international recognition he gained for Italy during the 1930s. If only for this motive he is still seen as a great man; we have already noted the way Gianfranco Fini (Berlusconi's foreign secretary for a time) put it. For Fini, Mussolini was 'the greatest statesman of the twentieth century'.

Hitler—the one mistake?

Among those disposed to give Mussolini the benefit of the doubt—
the 'after all, he did many good things' people—there is a constant
refrain: the Duce made one mistake and that was the alliance with
Hitler which determined Italy's entry into the Second World War.
Some have even suggested that, had it not been for the disaster of the
war, Mussolini would be up there with Mazzini, Cavour, and Garibaldi
as one of the great national heroes. In other words, if Mussolini had
not miscalculated and had kept out of the war, Fascism would have
been all right. This kind of mental balancing act—the plural positive
of the 'many good things' against the singular negative of the 'one
mistake'—has a comforting effect for those who engage in it. It effectively rescues Fascism, as peacetime regime, from condemnation. By
implication, if there is only one mistake, the rest of the history of the
regime cannot be considered a 'mistake'. Therefore—the suggestion is
clear—it can be seen as acceptable. The 'one mistake' becomes relative
and the door is left open for the appreciation of the 'realizations' of
the regime and of those who were responsible for those apparent
achievements. At this point, all things considered, Fascism can be seen
in a favourable light. Through an impressive process of wishful thinking we are once again on the road to self-forgiveness; OK, it finished
badly, but for the rest, Fascism was not really so bad. After all, we all
make mistakes and we hope not to be judged by those mistakes. Why
should we view Mussolini any differently?

We might begin by recognizing the measure of the 'one mistake'.
The cost for Italy was enormous and this cost has to be laid at the door
of the regime. Strangely, it is rarely remembered that the fascist war—
the 'one mistake'—cost Italy, between military and civilian deaths,
perhaps 500,000 dead, possibly many more. And even when the dead
are remembered, the cause for which they died—at least until 1943—is
all too often forgotten. The farce of the 'parallel war' represented
by the invasion of Greece, is forgotten; and the humiliation of

North Africa—135,000 Italians made prisoner in just two weeks—is hidden behind a glorification of the subsequent defeat at El Alamein. The tragedy of the Armir[1] is remembered more for the heroic struggle of the soldiers on the Don and less for Mussolini's absurd insistence on sending them, as invaders, to Russia, against the wishes of Hitler. A further example is the case of Cephalonia,[2] without doubt a—once again—heroic resistance against the Germans at the moment when the alliances changed, but very few official commemorations pause to ask what the Italians were doing in the Greek island. No one seems to remember that the same soldiers had, up to that point, been fighting a very dirty war on the side of Hitler. Words such as aggressors or invaders are rarely heard in this invocation of martyrs for the father-land, even less the association with Fascism—as if the Italian Supreme Command had been somehow independent of the regime. Perhaps it might be appropriate to state more firmly that the massacre of Cephalonia was just one outcome of a disastrous fascist foreign policy, that the victims of Cephalonia were victims not only of the Germans but also of Fascism and of long-lasting Italian great power pretensions. Yet the impression is that this cannot be permitted. By defining the opposition to the Germans at Cephalonia as 'the first act of the Resistance' (Carlo Azeglio Ciampi), the relationship of those events to the regime is obscured. Anger is directed at the Germans, not at Mussolini. It seems that a partial and 'patriotic' memory, a persistent recourse to victimhood, must necessarily trump a wider historical reconstruction of this tragedy.

The cost of the 'one mistake' was also a bitter civil war within Italy, with its often bloody repercussions in the years immediately following 1945. Yet, that the civil war, with all its terrible consequences, was a self-inflicted wound, with a story that goes back well before

1. The Italian expeditionary force sent to fight alongside the Germans in Russia in 1941–3. The force was very poorly equipped and suffered horrendous casualties.
2. Units of the Italian army, stationed in Cephalonia, refused to hand over their weapons to the Germans when the armistice was signed in September 1943. After a prolonged battle, the Germans disarmed the Italians. More than 5,000 of them were then immediately shot.

1943, is rarely recognized. The emphasis on the Resistance blocks any memory of earlier years. Certainly the anti-fascist tradition has ensured that memory of the partisan battle against the fascist republic and against the Germans has remained strong, but, as we have already seen, there has been an increasing tendency to separate the partisan struggle from its much wider political context—that is, to celebrate an anti-Fascism without the Fascism. That this is illogical is obvious. Nonetheless it fuels a discourse—perhaps because it is centred around the war against the Germans—that obscures the full extent to which it was Mussolini's 'one mistake' that produced death and destruction throughout Italy.

All in all, it could be said that the enormous cost of the 'one mistake', if properly assessed, should be more than enough to condemn Mussolini. And yet this has not happened. Many remain ambiguous about the fascist leader; some are indulgent, others have more than a sneaking admiration. Because, it would seem, everything was going well up to that fatal decision. This kind of reasoning, which sees Mussolini making an error in June 1940, is often reinforced by the further argument we have outlined above—the more general view of the international role of fascist Italy in the interwar years. Here it is maintained that, as a result of fascist policies, Italy was respected abroad as never before. Foreigners admired the Duce. Almost without fail Churchill's periodic flirtation with Mussolini is often brought into the picture. It was a moment—the argument goes—in which the country had effectively become one of the great powers, thus finally realizing the ambition of many Italians from 1861 onwards. Mussolini—it goes on—was present at the major international conferences; indeed he was a key figure at many of them—Munich above all—where he appeared to be the broker of a peaceful conclusion to the conference. Moreover Italy had an empire and had moved nearer to her objective of dominating the Mediterranean. Yes, the defenders of Mussolini argue, in 1940 he got it wrong but, up to that point, he had raised Italy's international prestige and made the country a major

European player. Very different from the subordinate position Italy has generally occupied on the international scene in the years since 1945.

Mussolini 'the statesman' is a line of thinking that is slow to die.[3] It is part of the Mussolini myth, developed in the 1930s by the fascist movement itself and evidently not forgotten in some circles. It offers a simple and straightforward picture—first large-scale success, then failure because of a single error. What it does not show is, that failure—that one mistake—was, at the time, totally in line with the politics that had produced apparent successes in the 1930s. It is an argument that rests on the idea that Mussolini might have decided not to enter the war in 1940, in the same way as he, very reluctantly, chose a policy of non-belligerence in 1939 (Bottai records a Mussolini 'unhappy and mortified' by the decision[4]). But, given the circumstances of June 1940, which made intervention against the French look so attractive (at the price, as Mussolini put it, of only 'a few thousand Italian dead'), it was highly unlikely that this path of passivity would be followed for a second time. War was built into Fascism, as we shall see; Ethiopia and intervention in the Spanish Civil War cannot be passed unnoticed. Mussolini's decision in June 1940 was entirely in keeping with with the policies followed during the 1930s; from his point of view intervention was anything but a mistake. This is evident from the vantage point of hindsight, very obviously; even so it seems unrealistic to argue that Mussolini got it wrong in 1940 when there is really very little evidence to suggest that he might have got it 'right'. All the evidence points in the other direction. Remaining on the sidelines of a conflict that seemed almost finished would have meant renouncing the possibility of a spectacular victory—very important because a *European* and not an African victory—courting humiliation in the eyes of

3. For a long period in the 1990s, in some street markets in Italy it was possible to buy a kitchen apron with the face of the Duce (with helmet) on it and the slogan 'Mussolini statesman' printed in large letters under the face.

4. G. Bottai, *Vent'anni e un giorno*, Milan, Rizzoli, 2008, p. 152. Other memoirs of the time record Mussolini's immense frustration at not being sufficiently prepared to join the war in 1939.

Hitler, and (according to Mussolini) risking the reduction of Italy to a country in the second division. Those who argue that the fascist leader made a mistake should realize that, by 1940, Mussolini had already made his bed and had to lie on it. The origins of the errors, the miscalculations, lie along the path trodden throughout the 1930s and cannot be confined to the single moment of 1940.

Imperial illusions: Ethiopia and beyond

Mussolini's present-day admirers may point to the alliance with Hitler as the 'one mistake' but they seem to have few problems with the Ethiopian war—sometimes even referred to as the Duce's 'master-piece'. For these admirers, armed aggression against independent states is all right, it seems—after all, most European powers had done the same at one time or another. It is even better if your enemy is a soft target and you are on the winning side. The expansionism first fully evident with the invasion of Ethiopia provokes no embarrass-ment; it can be accepted (and, it would seem, then rapidly forgotten).

However, it would be a distortion of the facts to consider the fascist regime as expansionist only with the aggression against Ethiopia in October 1935. In reality Fascism was expansionist from the outset, breeding on the aggressive tones of the First World War but also exalt-ing many of the themes propagated by Italian nationalism in the dec-ade before the conflict. The Italian Nationalist Association, which joined with the fascist movement in 1923, had always had its eyes on the Adriatic/Balkan region (much of which had been promised to Italy in the 1915 Treaty of London) and reacted vociferously to the terms of the Treaty of Versailles which, following the intervention of President Wilson, disregarded those promises. Mussolini himself, heavily influenced in the years immediately following the war by D'Annunzio, denounced the Versailles settlement in terms very simi-lar to the poet's 'mutilated victory'.

The view that Italy had won the war but lost the peace was exploited to the full. Few were left in doubt that Italy was fundamentally a revisionist power. At the same time, for much of the 1920s, Italy was in no position to do anything about it. The economic fragility of the country—a consequence of the war and of unprecedented levels of imports in the first half of the 1920s—made Italy dependent on loans from Britain and the USA and discouraged any kind of adventurous foreign policy which might have put those loans in jeopardy. In this period Mussolini, intent on consolidating his power within Italy, was, in the European context, more collaborator than contester, affirming Italy's negative view of the European settlement, affirming the importance of the fascist 'idea', but remaining within the limits imposed by diplomacy and negotiation.

The exceptions to this picture were represented by conflicts which the regime had 'inherited' from previous governments. The unfinished war in Libya,[5] where a brutal campaign of 'pacification' continued throughout the 1920s, was declared completed only in January 1932. It is estimated that at least 50,000 people died in Cyrenaica during the campaign, many in hastily constructed and poorly equipped concentration camps. In the same way, in the mid-1920s an even more brutal campaign was conducted in Somalia, where the fascist leader Cesare De Vecchi employed methods redolent of the worst type of blackshirt *squadrismo* against sultanates that had resisted Italian control. These operations remained outside the European framework, however, and did not alter Mussolini's fundamentally conciliatory attitudes in respect of the other great powers.

Two factors changed this situation. The first was the international financial crisis of 1929–30 which saw the withdrawal from Europe of American capital and the introduction of widespread policies of protectionism. An important consequence of the crisis was that

5. Between 1911 and 1912, Italy fought a war for the possession of Libya, at that point under Turkish control.

Italy became necessarily less dependent on foreign loans. Slightly paradoxically, Mussolini, with his position at home assured by the victorious Plebiscite of 1929 and the Lateran Pacts, found himself with a freer hand to further his expansionist ambitions.

The second factor was, of course, the arrival to power of Hitler in 1933, which had an enormous impact on so many aspects of fascist policy. The shadow of Nazism was to loom large in the following years, as Italian politicians and diplomats sought, often somewhat desperately, to affirm Italy's position as the first fascist power. In terms of influence within Europe, German ambitions to hegemony in the Balkan region were immediately evident, thus curtailing any possible Italian expansion in the region. While still fishing in muddy waters by supporting (and housing for a time, in Tuscany) the Croatian fascist, Ante Pavelic, Mussolini was forced to recognize that expansion in south-eastern Europe was no longer an option. Attention turned south, therefore, once again to Africa—and Africa meant Ethiopia.

If the fascist regime represents in many ways a black hole in Italian memory, the invasion of Ethiopia represents a black hole within a black hole. For many decades after the Second World War the Italian colonial experience was largely forgotten; the occupation of Ethiopia had been too short for it to leave any kind of conspicuous post-colonial legacy in the metropolitan country, compared to that in Britain and in France, and decolonization was itself very rapid. After the war, there were not large numbers of Ethiopians driving buses in Rome or cleaning Italian streets. In post-war years, as far as most Italians were concerned, Ethiopia might never have existed. Italy's image, following the war, was that of a peace-loving nation; the brutalities of conquest in Africa fitted badly with this self-image and were duly forgotten.

In more recent years historians such as Angelo Del Boca, Giorgio Rochat, and Nicola Labanca have attempted to bring the events of the 1930s back into focus, but all the evidence suggests that theirs is a decidedly uphill task. The invasion of Ethiopia takes second (more probably tenth) place to the Pontine Marshes in popular memory, and Mussolini is rarely seen as the dictator who, because of the Ethiopian war, which was a challenge to the League of Nations and represented an unprovoked attack on an independent state, played a fundamental role in upsetting the already precarious international stability of the 1930s.

As with the removal from national memory of Ethiopia, so too has the larger picture of fascist power politics of the 1930s been removed. This erasure of the war in Ethiopia from the national consciousness has created a serious lacuna of memory, not only because it then permits the consolidation of the myth of 'good Italians' but also because it removes all that the war encapsulates, in its inspiration and in its conduct, of so many of the ideas, attitudes, and practices that were characteristic of the regime itself. The aggression against Ethiopia was a culmination of fascist thinking. It represented the regime's quest for great power status and the belief that such status lay, for a European power, in the possession of colonies. It purported to respond to Italian needs for more space to respond to demographic pressures (with an assumption that much of Ethiopia was, first, cultivable; and, second, 'empty'). It represented a further example of the Italian 'victim' mentality—the idea that other nations had colonies and that these had been denied to Italy, first with the European powers' 'scramble for Africa' of the late nineteenth century, but also with the more recent settlement of Versailles. For these reasons Ethiopia was going to represent a settling of scores within Europe, the acquisition of something denied for decades to the nation. And, along with the final realization of great power status, the conquest of Ethiopia would also act to redress the 1896 humiliation of the defeat at Adua, a wound still festering in the nation's pride.

This is not the place for a detailed look at the Ethiopian campaign. Suffice it to say that it was a heavily orchestrated operation. With the eyes of the world on them, the fascists could not afford to fail. According to military historian Nicola Labanca, the military commitment was more suited to a world war than to a battle against a poorly armed enemy.[6] Moreover the conquest was carried out with a brutality that few have since acknowledged. Ethiopian military and civilian losses were enormous, Italian dead relatively few. Mussolini's eldest son—a pilot—described killing Ethiopians from the air in graphically delighted terms more suited to a hunting party than to a war. After decades of denial, their use of poison gas (prohibited by international agreement in 1925 but authorized on the direct instructions of Mussolini) has at last been officially admitted.[7]

The justification for the war, cooked up for domestic consumption, revealed a very clear racist element to the conflict. According to fascist propaganda, it was a war to bring Italian civilization to the backward and feudal Ethiopian Empire of Haile Selassie, a war to defeat a 'slave state'. In fact the invasion and subsequent occupation had few of the characteristics of a civilizing mission and many of those that typify colonial domination. Certainly, many building constructors and administrators made a fortune from the deviation of government funds. Even so, the fascist propaganda, still heard today in some neo-fascist circles, repeatedly boasted that Italian colonialism meant hospitals, schools, and roads, unlike the repressive and exploitative colonialism of other powers.[8] These there were, but in relatively small numbers when related to the costs. There were also numerous massacres of Ethiopians, the most notable being those following the attempted assassination of General Graziani in Addis Ababa in February 1937.[9]

6. N. Labanca, *Una guerra per l'impero. Memorie della campagna d'Etiopia 1935–6*, Bologna, Il Mulino, 2005.
7. On the massive scale of killing—hundreds of thousands—see M. Dominioni, 'La repressione di ribellismo e dissidentismo in Etiopia 1936–41', in L. Borgomaneri (ed.), *Crimini di guerra. Il mito del bravo italiano tra repressione del ribellismo e guerra ai civili nei territori occupati*, Milan, Guerini, 2006.
8. The myth of a 'benevolent' colonial power is, of course, common—to be found, for instance, in many accounts of British control of India.
9. It has been calculated that, following the assassination attempt, between 25,000 and 30,000 Ethiopians were killed in the course of three days, during which Graziani gave the Italian troops carte blanche to kill on sight. The massacre of 300 monks, suspected of complicity in the attack, and more than 1,000 pilgrims at the monastery of Debre Libanos took place three months later. See, for a recent evaluation, G. Finaldi, 'Fascism, violence, and Italian colonialism', *Journal of Holocaust Research*, 33, 1, 2019, pp. 22–42.

One very important aspect of the war and the subsequent occupation—an aspect people would prefer to forget—was that it was, as already stated, a racist war, with the Italian occupiers playing the role of the superior race in respect of an inferior indigenous population. While this did not prevent Italian settlers—administrators, soldiers, workers—from having families with local women and girls (called *madamato*; the famous Italian journalist Indro Montanelli 'married' a 12-year-old girl), it did constitute a problem for a regime which was, at least in theory, totalitarian, and therefore all-inclusive. Questions relating to racial purity became unavoidable. Was the indigenous Ethiopian population an integral part of the fascist state—the totalitarian solution—or was it to be excluded on grounds of race and colour? Was fascist Italy a political or an ethnic community? Squaring the circle was, in fact, impossible and the colony was too short-lived to see any definitive solution to the question. Nonetheless the discriminatory laws of 1937, intended to curtail the practice of *madamato* (and reduce the number of mixed-race children), did underline the distinction between the indigenous and the Italian populations, effectively creating a group of second class citizens within the totalitarian structure—an anomalous situation for a regime in which civil society was supposed to be subsumed by the state.

The issue, initially faced in the colony, was not to be without effect within Italy, because the efforts to categorize people according to race, the desire to avoid miscegenation, and the insistence on the need to ensure the 'purity' of the Italian people brought renewed attention to these distinctions within the metropolitan population, which would have fatal consequences in the years immediately following, as we shall see.

So was Ethiopia 'Mussolini's masterpiece'—a military and a diplomatic victory that finally gave Italy her rightful 'place in the sun' and rekindled enthusiasm for the regime at home? For a variety of reasons this positive view of the war would be questionable. An initial objection might be that the acquisition of colonies corresponded to a model of governance that other European powers were beginning to discard;

it represented a conception of power already out of date and really did little to build great power status. Furthermore, even ignoring this objection, it has to be said that Fascism's 'place in the sun' turned out to have little economic value. On the contrary, the Ethiopian war was a huge drain on Italian finances and provided little or nothing in exchange. More significant is the fact that, on a diplomatic level, international protest against this aggression was strong, with—ultimately—disastrous consequences from Mussolini's foreign policy. Italian isolation was marked by the imposition of sanctions by the League of Nations and this played a part in pushing Mussolini into the arms of Hitler—a long story, admittedly, and not without its twists and turns, but beginning in earnest at this point. As the ideological divisions became more marked, Mussolini's freedom of movement became more limited. This became even more obvious with what was, effectively, Italian intervention in the Spanish Civil War, when supposedly 'volunteer' blackshirt forces provided valuable support to the Spanish rebel forces (the units of the Italian air force having the dubious distinction of being, together with the Luftwaffe, the first to bomb civilian targets in Europe). The Ethiopian war played a large part in the formation of this fascist alignment.

Nor was the war the great success at home that it is often made out to be. Certainly the news that Italy 'had her Empire' was greeted with enormous enthusiasm and visions of economic (and sexual) exploitation flourished for a while. But the evidence suggests that this enthusiasm was very short-lived. Within weeks of the announcement of victory we find that police informers are no longer talking about popular enthusiasm but recounting the dissatisfaction of people with the difficulties they had to face in daily life. Unemployment, rising prices, corruption among officials—all the usual complaints returned to the foreground. Scepticism about the war had always been present in some quarters, with some arguing (rightly) that the money spent on the war would have been better spent at home and others doubtful (rightly) about the alleged value of the coveted colony. The man who suggested that, if Ethiopia had been worth anything, 'the British would already have got it' was not so wide of the mark. According to many reports, in December 1935, resentment at the requisition of 'gold for the fatherland' in order to pay for the war was widespread, with many resorting to ruses to avoid handing over valuable possessions (the purchase of a cheap wedding ring, to donate in place of the real one, was a common strategy).[10] All in all, popular opinion seems to indicate reservations about the conflict. Those who volunteered to go to Ethiopia were all too often 'unemployed, starving, ne'er do wells' according to one observer (a shopkeeper from Brescia)—people who saw the Empire as their future. That this future did not materialize as hoped is increasingly evident in the second half of the 1930s as it became obvious to everyone (with the exception of the many who managed to divert large sums of public money into their own private pockets) that the promised Eldorado of Africa was a profound disappointment. This was, perhaps, an inevitable reflection of the fact that Mussolini had wanted to have colonies, but had spent little time thinking about what they were for. Taking the long view, the whole operation was hardly a masterpiece.

Anti-Semitism, racism, and the racial laws

If Italian expansionism, Ethiopia, and the colonial experience have been so completely removed from popular memory (together with the several hundred thousand African dead), the same cannot be said for the racial laws of 1938–9. Every year, in the *Day of Memory*, homage is paid to the many Italian Jews who were deported to the Nazi camps, most of whom never returned. Auschwitz has become a more powerful symbol than it was fifty years ago. In many cities the 'stumbling stones', set in the pavement, are becoming a familiar sight, recording

---

10. P. Terhoeven, *Oro alla patria. Donne, guerra e propaganda nella giornata della Fede fascista*, Bologna, Il Mulino, 2006. But for the many attempts at avoiding the concession of the ring, see P. Corner, *The Fascist Party and Popular Opinion in Mussolini's Italy*, Oxford, Oxford University Press, 2012, pp. 192ff.

Italian Jews who were arrested, deported, and murdered. No one can say that the racial laws are not remembered.[11]

It is how they are remembered that is significant, however, because the memory of the racial laws has become more associated with Nazism, with Auschwitz, and with the Shoah than it has with the fascist regime.[12] Students are taken to Auschwitz and often remain in ignorance of the Italian camps, like Fossoli, which served as staging posts for the fateful journey.[13] A comforting theme has always been that Mussolini was only following Hitler's lead, given—it is said—that Italians have never been anti-Semitic. It is almost as if it is really just a German problem; once again the ball is knocked into the other court. One or two notable Italians who saved Jews are invoked in order to put the Italians among the Just. After all, the argument goes, before 1943 we didn't hand over 'our' Jews and (the self-forgiving mechanism kicks in again) we saved many of them from a brutal destiny.

This last is true. There were Jews hidden by non-Jewish families at great risk to themselves, just as many Jews found refuge in Catholic institutions. And, in certain areas occupied by the Italian forces, the Italian commanders did refuse to hand over Jews to the Germans (although this had more to do with the desire to demonstrate autonomy of command in respect of the Germans than with sympathy for the Jews themselves).[14] No one puts this in question. However, it is only half the story—perhaps less than half. The point is, rather, that the responsibility for discriminating against the Jewish population in Italy, with setting it apart from the rest of society and identifying it through registers (many of which would fall into the hands of

11. On the paradox of increasing attention to the Shoah and, at the same time, a currently increasing xenophobic racism, see V. Pisanty, *La difesa della razza. Antologia 1938–1943*, Milan, Bompiani, 2006.

12. See M. Sarfatti, *Gli ebrei nell'Italia fascista*, Turin, Einaudi, 2000; E. Collotti, *Il fascismo e gli ebrei. Le leggi razziali in Italia*, Rome-Bari, Laterza, 2003. For a concise and comprehensive account, see S. Duranti (ed.), *Leggi raziali fasciste e persecuzione antiebraica in Italia*, Milan, Unicopli, 2019.

13. On Italian camps, see C. S. Capogreco, *Mussolini's Camps. Civilian Internment in Fascist Italy*, London, Routledge, 2021 (orig. Italian 2004).

14. Collotti, *Il fascismo e gli ebrei*, pp. 117–19.

the Germans with murderous consequences), lay with the Italian government. Discrimination was not introduced at the behest of Hitler, even if the German example was no doubt very present in Mussolini's mind (in part because he was aware of the support anti-Semitism attracted for the German leader at the international level). It was done because it was coherent with a radicalizing fascist ideology—an ideology that, reflecting the African experience of a colonial population, was increasingly concerned with questions regarding the realization of racial purity and the cohesion of the Nation and with the expulsion of those elements that contradicted or corrupted these objectives.

Certainly, it should be remembered that the first Fascism of 1919, in Venezia Giulia, had expressed a radical and racist anti-Slav sentiment.[15] Moreover, there had always been an explicitly anti-Semitic group within the fascist ranks—Farinacci was a prime example, Interlandi another, and the defrocked priest Preziosi yet another—but these figures were not the determinants. What were determinants were those purely endogenous factors relating to the Nation and the constituent elements of that Nation, evidenced in the argument that Jews, because of supposed foreign allegiances, could never be fully 'Italian' and therefore never fully committed to the objectives of the totalitarian state. Fascism rejected diversity of all forms because diversity represented a challenge to the total, organic unity of the state. It was fascist totalitarian pretensions that eventually condemned the Jews, not Nazi pressures, as many would prefer to think. The Italian Jews fell foul of the totalitarian thrust.

But why in 1938? Why not before? The African experience was undoubtedly a catalyst, a moment of increasing clarity on what constituted an Italian and what did not; the question of 'national characteristics' came to the fore as never previously. But the racial laws were also functional to the regime in the sense that identifying a new 'internal enemy' (socialism was no longer a problem) was part of the

15. On the Fascism of the Italian eastern borders, see A. M. Vinci, *Sentinelle della patria. Il Fascismo al confine orientale 1918–1941*, Rome-Bari, Laterza, 2011.

process of further consolidating the regime around themes that denounced any kind of diversity. The discriminatory laws established a fresh division between 'We' and 'Them' and offered a much-needed element of dynamism to a regime that, by the late 1930s, was stagnating, with ageing leaders and often increasingly meaningless routines. Italians were invited to become energized against a common enemy. Moreover the anti-Semitic propaganda that accompanied the laws corresponded well with the international outlook of the regime—with Jews being identified on the one hand with democracy and capitalism (Blum, Rothschild) and on the other with Bolshevism (Marx, Luxemburg, Trotsky), the great external enemies of Fascism.

Far from being in some way an unfortunate side-effect of Mussolini's relationship with Hitler, therefore, the racial laws belong very firmly to the thought and practice of the regime itself. They were far from being an external imposition for which the Nazis can be blamed, even if the influence of Nazi thinking (along with other currents of contemporary European anti-Semitism) can be detected in certain of the main theorists of Italian racism. Nor is it possible to sustain the frequently heard argument that Italian anti-Semitism was in some way less obnoxious than that of the Germans—that it was 'spiritual' rather than biological. If fascist racism appears to differ from that of the Nazis, this has more to do with the need felt by the Italians to distinguish themselves from their dominating German partners than for any more substantial reason. Transnational pressures meant that, from 1933 onwards, Italians—the first fascists—were anxious to assert their primogeniture and demonstrate that, in respect of Hitler, the tail was not wagging the dog. It is enough to read the pseudo-anthropological, pseudo-biological nonsense of Giorgio Almirante ('Our racism has to be a racism based on blood') and Guido Landra, who advocated the 'elimination' of the 'worst elements' in the population, published by La Difesa della Razza to understand the immense efforts made to claim that Italians, in the hierarchy of races, were at the highest point of evolution—Aryans, exactly like the Germans (if not better). And La Difesa della Razza was not an insignificant scandal-sheet for fanatics.

No less a figure than Giuseppe Bottai ordered, as Minister of Education, that it be deposited in all university libraries and read, studied, and commented by professors and students alike.[16]

The racial laws cannot be fitted into that category of 'Mussolini's mistakes'—because the racism of Fascism exemplifies and unites so many of the threads that characterize the regime itself. Racism was related to war—as we have seen, a fundamental theme of fascist ideology. According to the racist theorists of the regime, a healthy, racially pure nation was inevitably expansionist—it was a question of survival among other competing nations—and war was the test of the 'quality' of a nation; a racially pure nation would always defeat a contaminated people. For the racists, the surprisingly rapid defeat of France in 1940 was the proof of this. France, according to Interlandi, had been 'eaten away from the inside, just as the invisible termites devour the middle of tree trunks', by Jews and people of mixed race.[17] Reasoning of this kind compelled some to look closely not only at the quantity of the Italian population—a constant preoccupation of the regime—but also at its 'quality'. As with animals, it was argued, just as coupling thoroughbreds with inferior stock produced bad results, so the mixture of bloods—Italian with Jewish or African blood—could only have deleterious results for the nation. Thus war, hierarchy of nations, demography, eugenics, anti-Semitism, and racism found their place together in a mishmash of theories that enlivened the daily operations of *Demorazza*.[18] Those fascist gymnasts of Rome who—as police reported—when passing the synagogue and seeing Jews coming out shouted 'Burn them', had already formed a clear idea of what fascist racial policy implied.[19] Yet we still find advocates of a 'benevolent Fascism'.

16. Pisanty, *La difesa della razza*; for the quotations pp. 56, 80.
17. Ibid., p. 107.
18. Ministero dell'Interno, Direzione generale per la demografia e la razza (formed July 1938)—the department responsible for putting the racial laws into effect, known as *Demorazza*.
19. Corner, *Fascist Party*, p. 230, note 13.

From 1938 onwards, fascist policies and attitudes pushed nearly 7,000 Italian Jews slowly but surely in the direction of the Shoah. Because, before 1943, there was no direct collaboration between Italy and Germany in the processes of extermination, Italian responsibility has always been fudged. In respect of the Shoah, 'We didn't know' has been the standard position.[20] While this is true of the population at large (although rumours of Nazi ill-treatment of Jews were widespread from the beginning of the war), at official level there is now no doubt that Mussolini and the senior fascist leaders knew fairly precisely what was going on from mid-1942 and made no moves to challenge German policies. It seems they were judged the less-than-acceptable face of an unloved ally, but the issue remained at that point. With the creation of the Repubblica Sociale Italiana in 1943 fascist attitudes hardened. Anti-Semitism became one of the cardinal features of government policy, with the Jews, now deprived of Italian nationality through the Manifesto of Verona, classified as enemies of the state with all the consequences that flowed from that definition. Hunting down Jews, betraying those in hiding, expropriating their property became activities accepted by the authorities; violence was common. None of this would seem to justify the bland self-justification of Italian innocence, the desire not to come to terms with this unpalatable past, which characterizes so much of Italian memory. Even less can it be allowed for Mussolini to be spared from responsibility—a partial responsibility—for one of the great crimes of the twentieth century.

Preparing for war, fighting a war

We rarely see the photos of a gaunt, defeated Mussolini, clad in a great-coat that looks several sizes too big for him, being greeted by a

20. As that remarkable Israeli historian, Otto Dov Kulka, has observed many times in relation to German popular opinion, 'We didn't know' does not mean 'We didn't want'. On popular opinion in respect of the racial laws, see V. Galimi, *Sotto gli occhi di tutti. La società italiana e le persecuzioni contro gli ebrei*, Firenze, Le Monnier, 2018, in which she questions the traditional view of the 'indifference' of the population.

jubilant Hitler after his rescue from the Gran Sasso in July 1943. Instead Mussolini with steel helmet, his chin thrust out in affirmation of masculine prowess, is a familiar picture. This is the warrior, the man who made others respect Italy, the man who challenged the existing order in the name of a greater Italy. Certainly, he got it wrong, he failed, but it was glorious all the same. We can still celebrate the heroes of El Alamein, the courage of soldiers walking back to Italy from defeat on the Don. After all, they fit beautifully the trope of the heroic victim.[21] And without much trouble we can divorce these events from the responsibilities of Fascism. The myth of Mussolini still works magic in some minds.

One of the paradoxes of the fascist period of rule is that the regime talked all the time about war, militarized society to a degree never seen before, assumed an aggressive pose on the international stage, emphasized constantly the need for personal sacrifice, but then performed so badly when it came to war itself. The attempt to create a permanent war mentality in time of peace had foundered somewhere. As Mussolini himself was bound to recognize in his last years, the fascist 'new man' had been tested and found lacking (perhaps more missing than lacking). The war had been a disaster. For the Duce, this was, of course, the fault of the Italians and not his; the dictator was the victim of those he had dominated for so long.

So, why military disaster? As emphasized in other sections of this book, it is not possible to separate the single issue—in this case, the performance of the military—from the overall picture of the workings of the regime and the objectives of Fascism. The single and the general are intertwined. To understand this it is sufficient to ask the question: why were the Italian units at El Alamein forced to fight with poor, outdated equipment? Or another, related question: why, shortly before his death in the skies over Tobruk, did Italo Balbo, finding

---

21. Not only victims of war, of course. The soldiers are also painted as victims of the Germans who, according to popular 'memory' used the Italians as cannon fodder in Africa and, in Russia, prevented Italians from retreating on the lorries loaded with German troops. Again, responsibility is directed away from Mussolini.

himself dramatically outgunned by the British in North Africa, have to telegraph Mussolini, asking him to procure some German tanks— far superior to the Italian tanks with which he was fighting at that time? It was not that Italy lacked brilliant designers and engineers. Even granting the limited resources available to the country, something had clearly happened in the move from bellicose rhetoric to military realization.[22]

The relationship between the military and the regime has traditionally been seen as one of relative distance, with the army loyal to the king rather than to Mussolini, and sometimes wary of a militarization of society that seemed, in certain respects, to create roles that reproduced those of the army. The fascist militia (MVSN) was the most obvious case of such reproduction. This presumed 'innocence' of the army (rather like the 'innocence' of the Wehrmacht until the 1995 Hamburg exhibition destroyed that myth) must be revised to some extent, however. It is clear, for instance, that the army played a role in the advent of Fascism to power. There was often very obvious sympathy between soldiers and blackshirts, both because of a common experience of war and because of an ideological disposition towards authority. Who was going to shoot at men who sported their war medals as they moved against the socialist leagues? Memoirs written by blackshirts speak of the stop at the army barracks for weapons before their attacks on socialist offices, with a further stop to hand back the guns once the action was over. This kind of collaboration was shown again in encouragement given to the first *fasci*. In his recent research on the role of the army in 1920–1, Gerardo Padulo has documented the complicity of the Ministry of the Interior, which was, in effect, in the winter of 1920–1, sending army officers on missions to stimulate the formation of *fasci* in provincial towns.[23] This may have been more unofficial, personal activity than due to official army

---

22. G. Rochat, *Le guerre italiane 1935–1943. Dall'impero d'Etiopia alla disfatta*, Turin, Einaudi, 2005, in particular pp. 251-54 for a concise judgement on fascist lack of preparation.
23. G. Padulo, *L'ingrata progenie. Grande guerra, massoneria, e origini del fascismo (1914–23)*, Siena, Nuova Immagini, 2018, p. 165.

policy; what is certain is that Victor Emanuel, on the occasion of the March on Rome in October 1922, decided that it was better not to ask the army 'to do its duty'.[24]

In theory, therefore, the advent of Fascism to power should have been favourable to the armed forces. Fascism and at least some elements within the military were on the same side. However, if war was certainly central to fascist thinking about the future of the Nation, ironically, this centrality did not always involve the army directly. Here it is important to remember that the militarization of Italian society under Fascism was not carried out by the military but by the civil authorities, to some extent pushing the military to one side. Mussolini with his helmet was the expression of this—the civilian dressed up as the soldier, the civilian who gave orders to the soldiers. Further, it has to be borne in mind that, throughout the *ventennio*, the king was constantly upstaged by Mussolini. In formal occasions it was always the Duce in pride of place, with the king playing a very modest supporting role. Mussolini drove the tanks, piloted the aircraft, and dominated at parades; Victor Emanuel either shared the podium or just looked on from a distance. The most powerful referent of the armed forces was weakened, therefore, which meant an accompanying weakening of the capacity of the armed forces to intervene in political decisions. It was no accident that, apart from a brief interruption, up until 1943 Mussolini took the ministries of the armed forces for himself. Thus decisions coming from these ministries were fascist decisions; they demonstrated all the usual deformities of such decisions in which political convenience took precedence over professional competence.

The inadequate preparations for participation in the Second World War were in part related to these priorities. While it is true that the intervention in the Spanish Civil War and, more particularly, the immense effort of the Ethiopian aggression, had been costly for the

24. On complicity between the military and the *squadristi*, see M. Mondini, *La politica delle armi. Il ruolo dell'esercito nell'avvento del Fascismo*, Rome-Bari, Laterza, 2006; also G. Albanese, *La marcia su Roma*, Rome-Bari, Laterza, 2006.

armed forces in terms of equipment, forcing Mussolini to tell Hitler that he would be ready for war only in 1943, the fact remains that the equipment being produced was often technically obsolete and of poor quality. Two factors should be noted in this regard. The first is that those industries producing armaments—here we are talking principally of Fiat, Ansaldo (which controlled Armstrong), and Terni—formed a kind of cartel following the end of the First World War, reducing any element of competition between them. The modernization of military production was slow and only partial. Thus, because it was profitable to do so, Fiat and Ansaldo continued producing lightly armed tanks long after they ceased to be a serious challenge to the tanks of other nations. These industries were, notoriously, very much linked to the regime. Here the second factor appears. In many cases (but not that of Fiat) those appointed to direct military pro-curement were either not technically competent or more inter-ested in furthering their careers—or both. Careerism, clientelism, corruption—as we have seen, characteristics of the regime—all had their role to play.

Emblematic in this regard is the case of Ugo Cavallero, appointed in 1928, with Mussolini's approval, to the presidency of Ansaldo, where he remained until 1933. Cavallero, an officer in the First World War, had left the army after the war and become heavily involved with industries producing armaments. Not a technician, he was essentially a manager and a go-between, a point of contact between the various heavy industries. During his period as president it was discovered that warships and tanks had been produced by Ansaldo with inferior armour-plate, that naval artillery had been 'adjusted' to cover up ser-ious defects, and that other military equipment, commissioned by the state, was sometimes defective in both quality and operation. The sus-picion that Cavallero had sanctioned this poor quality production in order to fill his own pockets was never proved (the regime, and par-ticularly the Ciano family, to which Cavallero was closely linked, pre-ferred to avoid the scandal) and he went on to have a distinguished military career—and, according to many, he also went on filling his pockets whenever he could.[25]

This might seem a straightforward story of the intertwining of industry and state, of shady business deals, corruption, and cover-ups, a story typical of a flawed and dysfunctional fascist regime that operated through personal contacts and a network of private interests. It bears note, however, that incompetence, political criteria, and corruption had their cost. Not only were Italian soldiers hopelessly outgunned at Tobruk and at El Alamein, but, because the shells produced by Ansaldo were defective, Italian naval gunners never managed to hit a British warship with their large-calibre guns in the entire course of the war.[26] It is hardly necessary to underline the fact that many Italians died because of this superficiality.

Yet the myth of Mussolini the warrior persists. Memory prefers myth to the historical record. In fact Mussolini seems to have been more interested in the appearance of military might than in its reality.[27] The armed forces were one element of his balancing act between the various centres of power within Italy and they were treated more from the point of view of political than of military power. The military were a political tool; efficiency was a secondary consideration. An excellent example of this came with Italo Balbo's appointment as governor of Libya in 1933. Resigning from his post as Commander of the Airforce, Balbo wrote to Mussolini that he was consigning 3,000 aircraft, of which only 1,900 were operational—hardly a brilliant

---

25. For further details, see L. Ceva and A. Curami, *Industria bellica anni trenta*, Milan, Angeli, 1992. Despite (or possibly because of) personal links, Ciano had no illusions about Cavallero's honesty; see *Diary 1939–43*, 6 July 1942: 'There is no question about it, Cavallero may not be a great strategist, but when it is a question of grabbing, he can cheat even the Germans.'

26. See P. Ferrari, 'Ugo Cavallero tra industria e stato maggiore', in M. Palla and P. Giovannini, *Il fascismo dalle mani sporche. Dittatura, corruzione, affarismo*, Rome-Bari, Laterza, 2019, p. 106.

27. This is the conclusion of the most recent study of Mussolini as military leader. See J. Gooch, *Mussolini's War. Fascist Italy from Triumph to Collapse (1935–43)*, London, Penguin, 2020.

result. Mussolini made his own checks and reduced the latter figure to
911. Nonetheless, he wrote that the situation was 'satisfactory' while
very clearly noting it as a weapon he could use against Balbo in the
future if necessary. Politics dominated, efficiency less so.[28]

In a sense, the conduct of the war reflected the same criteria. The
regime that had always been based on the supposed force of will
(*volontà*) found it hard to come to terms with the reality of conflict.
Ideological conviction had been a surrogate for effective military
strength and was soon found wanting, as Italian soldiers discovered to
their surprise when faced with Greek resistance and the hard truth
that Greek bullets killed as effectively as fascist bullets. They—some
of them volunteer university students—learned that the inspiration
of 'believe, obey, fight' worked better in peacetime than it did in a
real war.

The rest is well known. Greece, North Africa, the Russian front,
Yugoslavia—a chapter of disasters with few points of relief. The 'parallel war' of the Mediterranean turned out to be a humiliation. Mussolini,
as a commander in chief who did intervene actively in military decisions, must take much of the responsibility. His insistence, in the face
of Hitler's objections, on sending a poorly equipped Italian force to
the Russian front is a prime example—and here again the political
arguments outweighed the military realities; Italy had to be present in
the fight against Bolshevism, cost whatever it might. This campaign—
indeed all the Italian campaigns—demonstrated the fragility of the
regime and made evident those problems of organization and efficiency we have examined above. The tendency to overestimate Italian
power and underrate that of possible enemies had been built into the
rhetoric of imperial Fascism, particularly after 1936 when the regime
was ever eager to seem the equal of Nazi Germany. Many knew of
Italy's lack of preparedness for war but the imperative to feature on
the international scene remained too strong. Only Balbo, with his 'It
will be tough, very tough. We're not up to fighting a war seriously',

28. G. Rochat, *Italo Balbo*, Turin, UTET, 1986, pp. 230–33.

spoken under his breath to Bottai, seemed to have some idea of the real problems that lay in wait.[29]

A final, more general, consideration is in order. In Italy, popular memory of the war tends to highlight courageous defeats; El Alamein, the Don, Cephalonia, are all cases in point. The national narrative is that, even if betrayed by politicians and sometimes by generals, ordinary soldiers behaved well and as the situation required. All of which may be true. However, this 'personalization' of the battles has meant that certain moments of the war seem to have been removed from memory. The Italian occupation of mainland Greece, with ferocious anti-insurgency activities and the establishment of concentration camps in which many died of hunger, was hardly exemplary. Italian activities against partisans in Yugoslavia under generals Robotti and Roatta involved mass executions and extremely brutal reprisals against civilians. Roatta's battle cry 'Not a tooth for a tooth but a head for a tooth' has gone down in history.[30] Within Italy, as has become clear in recent years, Italian fascist troops and spies were often present at the many 'German' massacres that occurred among Italian civilians between 1943 and 1945, either killing directly or helping to identify those who were to be killed.

In recalling these episodes the intention is not simply to condemn; it is to underline the fact that their removal from popular consciousness serves to give a distorted impression of the fascist war. This has consequences. The Italian war is compared with the German war; in the first the crimes are forgotten, in the second they are always in the foreground. The good, humane Italian has become a cliché, and it is a cliché that has currency precisely because of a partially distorted comparison with that of the Germans. As Filippo Focardi has shown, in popular memory the Italian Second World War has become the great

29. Bottai, *Vent'anni e un giorno*, p. 186.
30. D. Rodogno, *Il nuovo ordine mediterraneo. Le politiche di occupazione dell'Italia fascista in Europa (1940–43)*, Turin, Bollati Boringhieri, 2003.

vehicle of the myth of 'the good Italian'.[31] Such a myth is in itself a simplification and in part, as Yugoslavia shows, an illusion, but it has the further effect of encouraging that kind of national self-pardon that pushes all the evil into the camp of the Germans and acquits the Italians. 'Fascism was not Nazism' rides again. True, but, as we have seen in Chapter 1, from here the road is short to the absolution of Italy—victim of the 'one mistake'—and from this point to the self-serving absolution of what then appears to be an innocuous Fascism. The lesser evil becomes no evil at all.

31. F. Focardi, 'La memoria della guerra e il mito del "bravo italiano". Origine e affermazione di un autoritratto collettivo', *Italia contemporanea*, 2000, pp. 220–1. F. Focardi, *Il cattivo tedesco e il bravo italiano. La rimozione delle colpe della seconda guerra mondiale*, Rome-Bari, Laterza, 2016 (3rd edn).

6

Mussolini as modernizer

A developmental dictatorship?

There is a persistent idea that dictators get things done. Whatever else is said about Stalin, many would not contest that he dragged Russia, and the rest of the Soviet Union, into the twentieth century. The cost in human lives was enormous but the economy developed at a speed rarely seen anywhere—sufficient, in fact, to permit the USSR to withstand and eventually defeat the Nazi (and fascist) invasion. Here, as often happens, dictatorship is associated with a supposed efficiency. Unhindered by parliaments, bureaucracy, or regulations, the strong man can make things happen. Sometimes Italian Fascism is seen in the same light. A popular take on the Duce—part of the Mussolini myth—is that of 'Mussolini modernizer'. It is not just that, under Fascism, the trains ran on time;[1] the 'modernizer' concept is related more to the image of economic planning, to the belief that the regime was working hard, through a series of ambitious projects, to turn a backward and predominantly rural Italy into a modern state on a par with other European powers. 'Italy on the move' was the message

---

1. One of the most persistent stories related to the regime. It is difficult to know the truth because, very obviously, schedules can be adjusted to make punctuality easy. Witnesses and memoirs suggest that mainline express trains did arrive on time, partly because drivers were fined if they did not. Other regional trains seem to have been as unpunctual as is normal everywhere.

the Fascism of the 1920s communicated to many, both within and outside Italy, and elements of this message have remained with us today.[2]

The land reclamation schemes are the prime example, the trains on
time another. Italy, it seems, thanks to Mussolini, was on the road to
becoming a modern nation. It is as though a firm and inflexible
regime had necessarily produced progress and efficiency and—central
to this argument—that this had been the core objective of the regime.
Indeed such is the attraction of this image that an American political
scientist—A. James Gregor—has argued that Italian Fascism was a
deliberately 'developmental dictatorship' on the lines of Mustafa
Kemal Ataturk's Turkey, Lee Kuan Yew's Singapore, or Park Chung-
Hee's South Korea—that is, a dictatorship which suppressed slow and
messy democracy and used the strong arm in politics in order to
'catch up' economically with other more mature nations. This interpretation can be read as a favourable cast on dictatorship, seen as justified in terms of future benefits—the ends justifying the sometimes
draconian means. It assumes that 'modernization' is necessarily a
positive phenomenon. Gregor pushes his argument to the extreme,
concluding, effectively, that, without Fascism, there would have been
no Italian economic miracle.[3]

Post hoc, ergo propter hoc is a dangerous line of argument for historians and few have followed Gregor in his teleological assertions, at
least not precisely in those terms. Nonetheless, the question of the
regime's relationship with 'modernity'—itself an ambiguous concept—
has attracted a great deal of attention, with most commentators
no longer prepared to accept the once-conventional view that the
regime was simply a defensive reaction to the challenge of economic
and social change, an attempt to turn the clock back to more stable

2. *Italia in cammino* was the title of a well-known book by Gioacchino Volpe, published
in 1927.
3. A. J. Gregor, *Fascism as Developmental Dictatorship*, Princeton, Princeton University
Press, 1979. For a convincing rejection of the concept of developmental dictatorship in
respect of Fascism, see J. S. Cohen, 'Was Italian Fascism a developmental dictatorship?
Some evidence to the contrary', *Economic History Review*, 41, 1, 2008, pp. 95–113.

times or at least to stop the clock from ticking.[4] It is not without importance in this context that the regime (imitating the French Revolution) actually invented a new calendar, starting from 28 October 1922, the March on Rome, as year one of the 'Era fascista' (although it is also significant that the old calendar did not always disappear. Often two dates lived confusingly beside each other on letterheads.) This was a move that encapsulated fascist pretensions to have launched a new historical epoch.

Contemporary cultural studies, very rightly rejecting the idea that there was no 'fascist culture', have stressed the modernity of some of the art and architecture of the regime, while others have focused on the development of radio and cinema. The regime was certainly not averse to cultural products, as sometimes thought; indeed, the mobilization of intellectuals and artists in support of the regime constituted one of the real novelties of the fascist approach to power.[5] The 'soft power' of cultural penetration was one of the roads taken by fascist government with its programme of international recruitment through cultural institutes.[6] Controls on artists were few and Italian Fascism resisted the creation of an official art on the lines of Nazi *volkisch* romanticism or Soviet socialist realism. What was important was that these cultural products did not threaten fascist control; diversity within domination was perfectly acceptable, as Minister of Education Giuseppe Bottai would argue repeatedly.[7]

---

4. For a review of interpretations regarding modernity, see A. De Bernardi, *Una dittatura moderna. Il Fascismo come problema storico*, Milan, Bruno Mondadori, 2001.
5. For the links between intellectuals and politics under Fascism, see G. Turi, *Lo stato educatore. Politica e intellettuali nell'Italia fascista*, Rome-Bari, Laterza, 2002.
6. R. Ben Ghiat, *Fascist Modernities: Italy 1922–1945*, Berkeley and Los Angeles, University of California Press, 2001; G. P. Brunetta, *Storia del cinema italiana*, Rome, Editori riuniti, 1979; for the radio, see P. V.Cannistraro, *La fabbrica del consenso. Fascismo e mass-media*, Rome-Bari, Laterza, 1974. In more general terms, see S. Soldani and G. Turi, *Fare gli italiani*, Bologna, Il Mulino, 1993. But see also the critical essay of D. Roberts, 'Myth, style, substance and the totalitarian dynamic in fascist Italy', *Contemporary European History*, 16, 1, 2007, pp. 1–36.
7. The exhibition in the Colosseum in Rome in 1984 (*L'economia italiana fra le due guerre*) attracted criticism precisely because it separated economic developments from their

The dangers of sectorial studies are very evident here. To argue that, if the art is modern, the regime is modern, is to extrapolate in an unjustified manner. In fact, most students of Fascism, recognizing this danger, end up by stressing the ambiguity of the movement—modern in some respects, traditional and conservative in others. And in certain policies it is not difficult to find elements of both. The famous invocation of the Duce in 1928 to 'ruralize Italy' is a case in point. While it might seem the expression of a desire to reject the evils of industrialization and reinforce traditional rural values—and undoubtedly there were elements of this in the policy—it answered at the same time to more immediate political concerns, being a pressing invitation to increase agricultural production at a time of growing international protectionism and—perhaps above all—an attempt to discourage the movement of labour to the towns at a moment in which politically dangerous urban unemployment was already increasing. It was, moreover, a reassuring ideological sop to a still-predominantly agricultural population, obliged to remain in an agricultural sector which, for many, meant extreme poverty.

Certainly the regime considered itself modern. Taking its cue at least partly from its futurist heritage, Fascism saw itself as a radical breach with the past, as the proponent of a new and exciting future. It portrayed itself as the regime of youth, as the regime building a fresh and energetic history for Italians—indeed, rather like communist regimes, as the very repository of history, constantly recruiting for the future. It repeatedly compared its supposed dynamism with the tired immobility of the exhausted democratic, 'plutocratic', and 'bourgeois', nations, struggling in the 1930s to come to terms with depression and economic crisis. Modernity, novelty, this was part of the affirmation on the European scene of a new Italy and a new Italian.

Undoubtedly there was much that was novel about Fascism, beginning with its relatively young leader, very different from the

political context. See, in particular, T. Mason, 'Italy and modernization', *History Workshop Journal*, 25, 1988, pp. 127–47.

grey-haired and ageing politicians who had preceded him. Mussolini the aeroplane pilot, Mussolini the racing car driver, Mussolini the sportsman—these were exhibitions intended to communicate modernity. Italo Balbo's crossing of the Atlantic with a squadron of flying boats sent the same message—a message received by joyous crowds in Chicago and New York. At home, prenatal clinics for young mothers and much-publicized camps by the sea and in the mountains for children gave the same idea of a new and modern state which embraced the concept of progress. And it was not all fascist window-dressing. Although still in a very limited way, more modern patterns of consumption were being established within Italy, principally among the growing urban population. Cinema meant that many Italians were increasingly fascinated by the American model, which could, of course, be envied, perhaps copied when possible, without accepting the American political system.[8] As we have seen in respect of relations of gender, more women were finding work outside the confines of the home, with inevitable changes in family organization. Education policy, as outlined by the Charter for the Middle School, showed a clear awareness of the needs of a modern capitalism. And for many there was the novel experience of leisure time activities. In all these ways there is little doubt that Italy was developing along lines similar to those of much of the rest of Europe, although at a slower pace and with many very pronounced regional differences.

In a further respect there was a clear effort at modernization. The fascist period saw a remarkable growth of state intervention in the economy through the creation of several hundred *enti*. These were

8. Officially the regime deprecated many Americanisms. On the parallel trends of attraction and revulsion in respect of the American model see D. W. Ellwood, *The Shock of America. Europe and the Challenge of the Century*, Oxford, Oxford University Press, 2012, in particular pp. 155–62; also V. De Grazia, *Irresistible Empire*, Cambridge, Mass., Harvard University Press, 2005; E. Gentile, 'Impending modernity. Fascism and the ambivalent image of the United States', *Journal of Contemporary History*, 1993, 1. On petty bourgeois behaviour and priorities, often more in vigorous defence of their own particular privileges than of fascist values, see Mariuccia Salvati, *Il regime e gli impiegati. La nazionalizzazione piccolo-borghese nel ventennio fascista*, Rome-Bari, Laterza, 1992.

public sector agencies with a large variety of responsibilities; there was an *ente* to control and regulate silk production, another with the same functions for the production of rice, another for projects regarding afforestation, another for the production of sugar beet, and so on. Many of them had a mainly technical function; there was, for example, and as we shall see, an *ente* responsible for the programmes of land reclamation. The expansion of these state administrative agencies was part of the centralizing and corporate thrust of government; all decisions were to be made by the Ministries in Rome and transmitted, through the public service agencies, to the provinces. As with the Party, what became known as the *parastato* of government agencies expressed the capillary vocation of fascist government, establishing a network of administrative control which grew in the course of the twenty years to employ more than 600,000 people.

Between them, state bureaucracy and the *parastato* exercised an enormous influence on economic activity, controlling flows of credit, levels of production, projects concerning industrial concentration, transport, public works, and so on. On paper the structure looked like a blueprint for dictatorial efficiency and it was certainly presented as such. It looked as though Rome would decide and, more or less immediately, Ravenna, Messina, Trento, Bari, or wherever, would respond with action. It looked modern; it looked managerial and not political. Again, it communicated the idea that, through its novel planned economy, Italy was on the move.

In many ways the creation of this structure was an impressive development. Certainly the numbers of those employed guaranteed a steady backbone of support for the regime that employed them. But, in terms of the characteristic that constitutes part of the dictatorial myth—efficiency—the picture is far less clear. As often happens with political projects in all kinds of government, but was particularly apparent with fascist government, there was an embarrassing gap between intentions and realization. The multiplication of agencies—more than 350 by 1940—produced an elephantine structure with a large number of overlapping and/or competing competencies. Rather than producing efficiency, the result was confusion and bureaucratic paralysis. As Guido Melis, the historian of the public administration, has shown, the 'machine' of public administration had gears that consistently failed to mesh.[9] Sometimes this was because of defence of position within the public administration itself—director against director—but on occasions it was also because of the interference of the Fascist Party. Public sector agencies were, at least theoretically, independent of the Party and exercised an influence which many local Party bosses resented. Putting a spoke in the wheel of public administration or, conversely, ignoring a recommendation coming from the Party became common expressions of the battle for local command. This was, at the local level, a further manifestation of the difficulties deriving from the competition between Party and state agencies, with the latter always defending very firmly their autonomy in respect of the former, and the former pushing all the time to penetrate areas which continued to escape its control.

None of this would prevent the regime from boasting its modernity in certain directions. The corporate state attracted attention, particularly among American political scientists. In ideological terms, as we have seen, the corporate state was conceived as a 'third way' of going forward, not of turning back—a 'third way' that envisaged a future neither capitalist nor socialist, an 'alternative modernity' to that offered by others.[10] It was this third way that was to permit Italy to dominate the twentieth century—'the century of Fascism' as Mussolini promised. But, if the corporate state is hardly remembered today, in part because it had little impact even within Italy, what has remained implanted in popular memory is the programme of land reclamation. Indeed, the main plank of argument for those who see Mussolini as a modernizer remains that of the land reclamation schemes—the *Agro Romano* (or Pontine Marshes) is always cited as an example of a successful

9. G. Melis, *La macchina imperfetta. Immagini e realtà dello Stato fascista*, Bologna, Il Mulino, 2019, ch. 4.
10. On the 'third way', see G. Santomassimo, *La terza via fascista. Il mito del corporativismo*, Rome, Il Mulino, 2006.

modernizing programme. It is a scheme sometimes accompanied by reference (for the more economically aware) to a further fascist 'invention'—the reorganization of the banking sector, with the creation of the Institute for Industrial Reconstruction (IRI), the state holding company that guided much of the Italian economy until relatively recent times and has often been held up, particularly in the 1960s, as a shining example of modern economic organization.

The Pontine Marshes: reclamation as a metaphor

Extensive land reclamation (*bonifica*) was one of the great propaganda weapons of the regime. As proclaimed by the authorities, land reclamation was going to eliminate disease-generating marshlands and provide vast new expanses of cultivable earth to be allocated to small proprietors who would then feed the burgeoning population. Thus reclamation was to serve multiple purposes, resolving land hunger among the peasants and helping the regime to move towards autonomy in the provision of food. More bread for more Italians was the underlying propaganda message. It was a message of triumphant modernization that had great force; after all, it was man mastering nature—a good fascist theme. Even today, the draining of the marshes represents one of the central elements of the favourable myth of Fascism. Tajani, when specifying one of the 'many good things' done by Fascism, immediately indicated land reclamation.

Land reclamation in Italy was, of course, nothing new. The immense marshlands of the delta of the Po, for example, had been drained and turned over to cultivation long before the First World War. The fascist project was, therefore, part of what was, in reality, an already ongoing programme; the initial project for the reclamation of the *Agro Romano*, for example, was drawn up in 1918, well before the advent of Fascism.[11]

11. In general, on land reclamation, see P. Bevilacqua and M. Rossi-Doria, *Le bonifiche in Italia*, Rome-Bari, Laterza, 1984.

What was new in the fascist programme (apart from the massive propaganda effort linked to it) was undoubtedly the extent of the project—millions of hectares to be reclaimed—and, above all, the idea of *bonifica integrale*—that is, not just the draining of the marshes but the division of the reclaimed land into small plots to be farmed by a new class of small proprietors and leaseholders. The intention was to reduce unemployment among the politically dangerous landless labourers and, at the same time, to realize the old conservative dream of the creation of social and political stability by fixing on the land people now directly interested in the results of their own production.

There were two phases to the scheme, therefore. The reclamation of the land was to be followed by a process of agricultural transformation, with the objectives of the transformation being not only economic but also political. It is to be noted, however, that the programme was not financed entirely by government funds. While the initial process of reclamation—draining and drying—was to be funded largely by the state, the subsequent process of agricultural transformation—the division of the land into smallholdings and the settlement of the peasants on these plots of land—was to be financed by the landowners themselves.

Associated with the name of the agronomist Arrigo Serpieri,[12] a reformer who had developed his ideas under Francesco Saverio Nitti, the programme was ambitious and had its undoubted successes—the showpiece Pontine Marshes being the best known. Foreign visitors were impressed by what looked like fascist modernizing vigour. Even with the Pontine Marshes, however, problems arose very quickly, with indebted peasants abandoning the land by the end of the 1930s in order to go to work (for cash) in Rome as waiters or building workers. This points to a failure of projecting. Where agricultural transformation had been effected, peasants were often settled on the land without adequate resources to buy seed and equipment and fell into debt

12. On Serpieri, see R. Tolaini, 'I contadini italiani e le loro famiglie negli anni trenta. Le ricerche dell'Inea di Arrigo Serpieri tra ruralismo e modernizzazione', *Quaderni storici*, 2, 2010, pp. 359–92.

before the land itself could begin to produce a livelihood. Applications to raise loans fell on deaf ears.

A greater problem for the project as a whole, however, lay in the reluctance of large landed proprietors to transform and divide their lands once they had been reclaimed. The law defining the programme had originally envisaged sanctions against reluctant landowners, including expropriation, but these sanctions were first toned down and then abandoned after 1934—understandably, from the point of view of the regime, because action against the landowners threatened to undermine one of the main sources of support for the regime. Expropriation of land, generating hostility among the landowners, would have been much like the regime sawing off the branch on which it was sitting. As a result, many landowners saw a great increase in the value of their land, reclaimed at public expense, while avoiding the cost of the further transformation expected of them. Only in 1940, with a law regarding the Sicilian *latifondia*, were moves made to enforce colonization of reclaimed territory.[13]

There was, as we have said, the usual gap between project and realization. Certainly, during the difficult economic conditions of the 1930s money for what were, in effect, highly labour-intensive public works programmes was very limited and this was reflected in the curtailing of many schemes. By 1940 less than half of the projects of reclamation had been realized, and less than half of the reclaimed land had been transformed as intended by the law. Some estimates put the figures much lower. Overall the reclamation projects favoured the North rather than the South and effects on production were marginal.[14]

The programme of land reclamation was, in short, a good idea done badly—and done badly not only because of lack of resources but at least in part because of the class bias of the regime. Serpieri resigned

---

13. S. Lupo, 'L'utopia totalitaria del Fascismo', in M. Aymard and G. Giarrizo (eds), *Storia d'Italia*, vol. V, Turin, Einaudi, 1987.

14. J. S. Cohen, 'Un esame statistico delle opere di bonifica intraprese durante il regime fascista', in G. Toniolo (ed.), *Lo sviluppo economico italiano 1861–1940*. Rome-Bari, Laterza, 1973, pp. 351–66.

from office in 1934 precisely because he could see that the regime was not prepared to risk support by putting his concept of agricultural transformation into action. Where radical action was required against the large landowners, the regime pulled up short. This underlined the tensions that existed between progressive economic policies and the conservative social base of the regime. It was a tension between intention and reality, between ambitious projects and the possibilities of realization, between radical ideas and social conservatism. As with the corporate project, fascist economic planning was always to suffer from this tension..

Economic planning: protectionism, autarchy, and state holding companies

Even those with only limited knowledge of the fascist period know that the state holding company, IRI, was an invention of the regime. Often this invention is seen as a feather in the cap of Mussolini, an example of far-sighted and original economic planning. It was, as everyone knows, IRI that played a large part in the economic miracle of the late 1950s and early 1960s. Here again we find the idea that there was modernization under Fascism, with heavy state intervention in the economy, and that this enlightened intervention produced institutions that would prove their worth in later years.

In few cases more than in that of IRI is it necessary to distinguish between intentions and results. If, with the land reclamation schemes, the grand intentions were belied by the mediocre results, with IRI the intentions were short-term and provisional, the results much more permanent. However, before returning to the specific case of IRI, a few words of context are necessary. These concern predominantly the question of the relationship between politics and economics under the regime. For much of the first half of the 1920s Mussolini was 'liberal' in orientation. The regime's first decisive interventions in the economy came with the 'Battle for Wheat' in 1925, intended to make

Italy self-sufficient in grain and obviate the need for expensive imports of wheat, and then, in 1927, with the revaluation of the lira. The so-called 'Quota 90' (ninety lira to the pound sterling) was determined by the justified need to stabilize the lira, but the overvaluation of the currency (many thought 120 more appropriate) owed much to questions of prestige, Mussolini being determined to show that the country had a strong currency. The immediate effect was deflationary and prompted the reductions in wages noted above. However—important for the fascist-orientated petty bourgeoisie—savings were effectively revalued. The longer-term consequences were the sacrifice of exports (textiles and agriculture) in the interests of those industries that imported raw materials from abroad. Among these were heavy industries—chemicals, metals, electricity—around which ideas of national self-sufficiency were beginning to develop. These were industries accustomed to the protection of the state and they were, very obviously, also industries connected with the production of armaments.

The slide towards autarchy was reinforced by the general world economic crisis of 1929 which, in a few words, forced Italy back on its own resources, encouraging policies of import substitution.[15] International loans were no longer available and the subordinate and dependent nature of the Italian economy was made ever more evident. From being an open economy in the 1920s Italy passed to being a closed and heavily controlled economy in the 1930s, with economic nationalism the guiding force—something which meant that the reasoning behind decisions would often be dominated more by nationalist than by economic thinking. An important caveat to this last statement, however, must be that, in particular during the 1930s, Italy saw the emergence of a number of competent economic managers—Beneduce, Menichella, Saraceno—who did little more than pay

15. Import substitution was possible only up to a certain point. Raw materials, which had to be imported, were paid for by dumping agricultural products in European markets. Such policies—much like the Battle for Wheat—saw inevitable distortions in agricultural production. On the quest for economic independence, see C. Scibillia, *L'olimpiade economica. Storia del Comitato nazionale per l'indipendenza economica (1936–37)*, Milan, Franco Angeli, 2014.

lip-service to the regime and were able to pursue a more enlightened economic strategy in certain areas.

The fundamental problem for Italy was the lack of capital, needed to further the process of industrialization. With the withdrawal of American loans and with the collapse of the stock market after 1929, several major banks in Italy either collapsed or seemed about to collapse, threatening to bring major industries down with them. This is the context in which first the Istituto Mobiliare Italiano (IMI, 1931) and then the more effective IRI (1933) were formed, initially as temporary institutions with the job of bailing out banks and industries in trouble and providing capital for relaunching. The central importance of IRI was fully understood only after its formation, when it became obvious that it was an instrument that permitted the state to intervene massively in the running of the economy. More through necessity than through judgement, one might say, IRI proved to be a formidable vehicle of state control, beginning life as the 'hospital for sick companies' but becoming, under Beneduce and Menichella, a permanent public authority in 1937.[16] Financed in large part through a 'plundering' of the reserves of INFPS (to the cost of contributors), by 1940 IRI held a controlling interest in large sections of Italian heavy industry, including those producing iron and steel, artillery, and shipbuilding—all of which were linked to production for war.

In reality, IRI was the most notable product of a vast process of reorganization of the Italian economy during the 1930s. It was a reorganization that saw an increase in state intervention, with an economy gradually subjected to a mass of controls and directives from ministries and government departments. Particularly important in the second half of the 1930s was the Ministry of Foreign Exchange, which, because of the shortage of foreign currency, determined, through the issue of licences, the nature and quantity of both imports and exports.

16. IRI functioned well. This may have been because it remained outside the arena of fascist politics. Beneduce employed competent financial technicians, many of whom were not linked to the regime, and, to the great surprise of many, blocked all political appointments. Beneduce himself took the Party card only in 1940 when appointed Senator. See Melis, *Macchina imperfetta*, p. 491.

As a consequence the political dimension of economic choices became far more prominent than it had been in the 1920s; it was what the state wanted that was decisive, not the wishes of the individual producer. This trend can certainly be interpreted as 'modernization' of a sort—economic *dirigisme* on the part of the state was a new phenomenon, provoked by crisis, and evident in other countries, Nazi Germany, the USSR under Stalin, and Roosevelt's USA being the most conspicuous examples. What is clear in the Italian case, however, is that the restructuring of the economy around the concept of autarchy obeyed those priorities of Fascism that we have seen earlier. The state intervention of the 1930s was conditioned by the criteria of the politics of power—expansion, prestige, and armaments—and tended to benefit certain industries and certain sectors of agriculture rather than others. In general, the industries favoured were heavy industries producing for the home market (often for the state) and large-scale, capitalist agriculture, which saw prices fixed to its advantage. Even so, controls were not always welcomed: as industrialists said at the time, 'The shirt [Fascism] is getting a bit too tight'. But complaints stopped short of opposition; state contracts and, above all, the rigid discipline of labour compensated abundantly for the inconveniences of a highly controlled and bureaucratic system.

Such modernization as took place—and certain industries, the chemical and electrical industries, for example, made notable progress during the 1930s—was unbalanced and favoured the strong rather than the weak, producing concentration rather than extension. This did not preclude technological progress (much of it imported, despite autarchy) but competition was limited, reducing the incentives for innovation. Private demand remained weak, as was inevitable with low wages and the compression of consumption, and the slow development of consumer industries reflected this. The regime defended profits, which remained high, but, with the state intervening so heavily in the management of the economy and with almost no pressure from wages, there was little stimulus to increase efficiency. Many government measures favoured the North rather than the South; fascist economic policy did nothing to close the gap between the two.

One point, in particular, should be noticed because of its ill-fated consequences. The commercial policies of the regime bound Italy more and more closely to Germany, with Germany taking a large proportion of Italian agricultural products in exchange for essential coal and iron ore—'coal for lemons' as it was dubbed at the time. Politically, this was an unequal exchange: Italy could not do without coal, Germany could survive without lemons. This was to weigh heavily in the decisions of 1939–40 when the level of dependence became evident, underlining the fact that policies of self-sufficiency could only go so far. This position of subordination was compounded by the fact that there were thousands of Italian workers in Germany, sent by agreement with Hitler in 1938–9, and they remained virtual hostages of the German leader.

Fascist policies were undoubtedly conditioned in part by the difficult international circumstances of the 1930s, but protectionism, state monopolies, state contracts, and state-organized bailouts of banks and industries in trouble did little to produce a dynamic capitalism. Economic policies reflected political decisions that were related less to economics than to criteria which had more to do with prestige, and often, in the final analysis, decisions were related more to will (*volontà* was one of the regime's keywords) than to reality. The determination to retain the overvalued lira until 1936, with its disastrous consequences for trade, was a case in point. Mussolini was given to making decisions on the basis of what he would have liked the situation to be rather than what it really was, preferring illusion to fact. As Alberto Aquarone has written, by the end of the 1930s the organization of the economy was characterized by confusion, parallel institutions, and overlapping departments, giving rise to the impression that what progress had been achieved was achieved more in spite of the regime than because of it.[17] This was the economic side of the 'politics of prestige'—hardly a model of dictatorial efficiency.

17. A. Aquarone, *L'organizzazione dello Stato totalitario*, Turin, Einaudi, 1965 (re-published 1995), ch. 5.

7

Mussolini

Myth and memory

Dictators love to be loved. Charisma both provokes and feeds on adulation. Even when there is no real personal charisma on offer—Stalin could be an example here—the appearance on the balcony to acknowledge the enthusiasm of the crowds does no harm to either leader or led. Both can feel satisfaction, knowing that they are in accord and united in their mission. This 'public' aspect of modern dictatorship points to the fact that effective political control depends to a certain extent on an active emotional relationship between ruler and ruled. Totalitarian control, to achieve its ends, requires more than passive conformity. Indeed, one of the 'tricks' of mass dictatorship is that of convincing the people that it is they who are determining events, that the dictator is doing no more than speaking on their behalf. Because of this, mass mobilization and popular participation are part of the recipe for successful dictatorship, to the extent that dictatorship might almost be called a collective enterprise. It remains, however, a collective enterprise in which all those features of negotiation and mediation now commonly identified in the relationship between ruler and population are heavily conditioned by the structures and the dictates of the regime itself. As we know well, apparent spontaneity is all too often a carefully constructed spontaneity; the regimented joy of parades in Pyongyang is obvious to everybody.[1]

1. On this 'collective' nature of totalitarianism, see 'Introduction' in P. Corner and Lim Jie-Hyun, *The Palgrave Handbook of Mass Dictatorship*, Basingstoke, Palgrave Macmillan, 2016.

An element in the careful construction of spontaneity is the personality cult—the creation of an aura of exceptional competence around the figure of the leader, presented as a person of remarkable vision, even as a kind of representative of destiny, in some way set apart from ordinary mortals. The cult exploits what is undoubtedly the fascination of extreme power. Very clearly, in the age of mass media, propaganda has a huge role to play in this construction; it is one of the most powerful factors in establishing the link between dictator and population. It is hardly necessary to dwell on this point. What is to be noted, however, is that the propagandistic self-representation of dictatorships—obviously positive, obviously extolling the virtues of the leader—seems to have a life that goes beyond the extinction of the dictatorship itself. While it is true that dictators move from great heights of public adulation to profound depths of popular loathing—we have touched on the cases of Stalin and Ceauşescu in Chapter 1—the myths they create around themselves while alive are rarely totally dismantled after death. Indeed, in some cases, with time, the myth itself becomes magnified. Nostalgia looks to these myths, which continue to have a hold because they have assumed a life of their own, usually divorced from the reality of the dictatorship itself. We still hear the cheers; we no longer suffer the strait-jacket of social control. The myth of Mussolini is just such a case.

Mussolini: the myth

We began this book by recalling the scenes in Piazzale Loreto in April 1945, with the body of Mussolini, bruised and bloody, suspended head down from the gantry of a petrol pump. The former dictator was subjected to a public execration that suggested the release of a long-repressed loathing and hatred. Yet this was the same man who had been glorified throughout Italy less than ten years before, who had found cheering crowds wherever he went. This was the man people fought with each other in order just to touch. He was 'the universal genius', the new Caesar, the 'national prophet', the embodiment of the New Fascist Man, and, of course, 'founder of the Empire'.

Such reversals of fortune are not uncommon in history, particularly for tyrants. And, as many dictators learn to their cost, cheering crowds are not to be trusted; they are fickle and can change humour from the morning to the evening. In his final years, Mussolini himself dwelt on this point, accusing the Italians of not being worthy of him, of having betrayed his aspirations for them. His disdain for a people that was 'too tender hearted' was expressed on various occasions. But what is surprising in the case of this fascist leader is that the spontaneous public vilification of Piazzale Loreto was in no sense the final act of the Mussolini saga. Unlike Hitler who, although remaining a figure of undoubted and enormous historical interest—witness the success of the television 'Hitler Channel'[2]—when once dead, remained dead, in the sense that few would now look back on him with nostalgia, Mussolini was very quickly resuscitated as a figure who continued to have some attraction. As Sergio Luzzatto has shown, the very body of the Duce became an issue in the immediate post-war, and by the early 1950s popular magazines were running articles on the Duce and his family, testifying to an ongoing fascination at popular level with the figure of the fascist dictator. Evidently, in some circles at least, the myth of the Duce continued to have its hold.[3]

This myth has had its ups and downs in ensuing years, but it now seems to have stabilized with a general, possibly slightly grudging, but often indulgent, acceptance. Mussolini was not so bad after all; there have been worse, etc., etc. And, as we know only too well, he did 'many good things'. The myth seems to have taken hold again. According to this narrative, Piazzale Loreto becomes almost an unfortunate incident, almost an embarrassing martyrdom, in the life and death

2. Popular name for the History Channel because of the amount of time it dedicates to the Nazi leader.
3. S. Luzzatto, *Il corpo del Duce. Un cadavere fra immaginazione, storia,e memoria*, Turin, Einaudi, 1998; for the 1950s, see C. Baldassini, *L'ombra di Mussolini. L'Italia moderata e la memoria del Fascismo (1945–60)*, Soveria Mannelli, Rubbettino, 2008.

of a man who was, despite defects and despite the 'one mistake', an impressive Italian.

It is as well to be aware of what is myth and what is reality, because, as this book has tried to show, so much of what is said and written about Mussolini corresponds more to myth than to reality. And the myth is, in large measure, the myth created by Fascism itself, not a subsequent elaboration of what Mussolini really represented, not a calculated reflection made with the benefit of hindsight. In other words, that artificially created 'cult of the Duce' which boosted Mussolini to such heights continues even today to colour his image. Although part of Fascism's own self-representation, it still remains a point of reference. For this reason it is worth looking for a moment at the origins and the characteristics of what was one of the first examples of the modern personality cult.

The cult was initiated only after the establishment of the regime—that is, after 3 January 1925 and the subsequent repressive legislation of the 'most fascist laws'. Before that time Mussolini had been to a great extent the first among equals, a politician among others. His personal magnetism was obvious and his charisma as a public figure was acknowledged but these were not decisive factors. Many of his close associates continued to give him the familiar 'tu' and it is significant that his lieutenants threatened to go ahead without him when he hesitated in the face of the Matteotti crisis at the end of 1924. It was only from 1926 that his position as an 'extraordinary' leader was established when Party secretary Augusto Turati purged and restructured the Party, creating a rigid hierarchy of command which put a greater distance between the leader and his followers and left few doubts about the exalted position of the Duce, who was now answerable only to the king and not to parliament. At the same time, Mussolini's personality was emphasized and exaggerated in biographies such as *Dux*, by Margherita Sarfatti (Mussolini's mistress for many years), which placed the fascist leader in a wider historical context and insisted on his extraordinary physical and mental capacities. As a man described as being truly exceptional, with a role to play in history, Mussolini was placed firmly outside the realm of ordinary men.[4] The Pope, Pio XI, played his part as well, with his 'Mussolini, man Providence'. For a Catholic country, this was some testimonial.

The Mussolini cult never reached the heights of that which surrounded Hitler. Hitler was the 'saviour' of the nation and the messiah leading Germany to her historical destiny after a humiliating defeat in the First World War, more than a decade of political confusion, and an immense economic crisis.[5] Mussolini did not have to satisfy such extreme needs. Nonetheless his cult was still, at the time, enormously important, because it incorporated more than anything else confidence and hope in the future. The cult reached its apex in the 1930s, largely through the operations of Party secretary Achille Starace. Radio, cinema newsreels, newspapers and magazines, public exhibitions, huge slogans on prominent walls—all helped in the propaganda exercise, extolling Mussolini's remarkable qualities and making him present to the population as no politician had been before him.[6]

Ever conscious of its place in history, the fascist movement represented itself as the culmination of a glorious Italian past, producing a new Rome, with Mussolini the new Roman emperor. At its pinnacle— probably around the proclamation of the Italian Empire in 1936—the cult painted Mussolini as omnipotent, virtually ubiquitous, and with a range of abilities that equalled those of the true Renaissance man.[7] He was the triumphant statesman, the modern Prince, envied

4. The classification of Mussolini as 'extraordinary' was a powerful feature of his charisma; see M. Weber, *Economy and Society*, New York, Bedminster Press, 1968, for the importance of the distinction between 'ordinary' and 'extraordinary' in the creation of the charismatic leader.

5. On the Hitler myth, see I. Kershaw, *The Hitler Myth. Image and Reality in the Third Reich*, Oxford, Oxford University Press. 2000 (re-edition); and I. Kershaw, *Hitler, the Jews, and the Final Solution*, Jerusalem, Yad Vashem, 2008, section II.

6. On the 'factory' of consensus, see P. V. Cannistraro, *La fabbrica del consenso. Fascismo e mass-media*, Rome-Bari, Laterza 1974.

7. See L. Passerini, *Mussolini immaginario*, Rome-Bari, Laterza, 1991. For examples of the extent of Mussolini-worship, see C. Duggan, *Fascist Voices. An Intimate History of Mussolini's Italy*, London, Bodley Head, 2013; also C. Duggan, S. Gundle, and G. Pieri (eds), *The Cult of the Duce. Mussolini and the Italians*, Manchester, Manchester University Press, 2013.

by other nations, at the same time at home with intellectuals with whom he could discuss philosophy on equal terms; as a man of the people, he was able to harvest wheat with the peasant without making a fool of himself. He was the Latin lover but also the perfect husband—the perfect mix for a sexist country that set so much store on the family. He was adventurously modern; he could drive fast cars, pilot planes, and tame lion cubs. He was thought to oversee everything. Legend said that he had been seen on a motorcycle at night, riding through the Pontine Marshes in order to ensure that everything was in place. He was indefatigable, working long hours in order to further the interests of the people. The light left burning late into the night in his office in Piazza Venezia was the evidence of this. And, of course, he saved ordinary people from the need to make stressful choices because, as the slogan insisted, Mussolini was always right.

Mussolini, always a brilliant showman, played up to this image all along the line. Nor did it finish there. As many commentators have stressed, there was a strong physical strand to the admiration of the Duce (and Mussolini made no secret of his virility), just as there were equally strong religious overtones in the language used to describe him. Indeed much of fascist liturgy overlapped with that of the Church—an important factor in a strongly Catholic country—and the fascist leader benefited from this religious association. In short, he was half saint, half film star—the true celebrity of his time.[8] As personal diaries show, his figure touched Italian sensibilities in a multitude of ways.[9] He projected strength, direction, and promise for the future. Above all, it was clear that, with Mussolini, Italy was at last on the winning side of history.

The amount of servile adulation that was reserved for him, even by close colleagues, is embarrassing to read and is almost unbelievable today. There seems to have been a contest among hagiographers to

8. One of the first to apply the world of the celebrity system to a reading of Italian Fascism has been S. Gundle, *Mussolini's Dream Factory. Film Stardom in Fascist Italy*, New York, Berghahn Books, 2013.
9. Duggan, *Fascist Voices*.

see who could use the most lavish superlatives. This is all the more surprising when it is considered that many of those adulators nearest to Mussolini must have been aware that they were reflecting what today would be called a cultural construct, ably engineered by experts in communication working from the 'factory' of consensus, and that the narcissistic and increasingly moody neurotic they had in front of them hardly qualified for the role of demi-god which the cult had assigned to him.[10] Nonetheless, while the fascist leader continued to have his detractors—Romans referred to him disparagingly as 'the big stink'—the cult clearly worked for many. Late in the 1930s commentators noted that, even though a lot of Italians might be fed up with Fascism and with the endless, pointless activities of the PNF, they remained in thrall of Mussolini. As one of them succinctly (and in a manner very revealing of the fragility of the regime) put it, 'Mussolini without Fascism is conceivable, Fascism without Mussolini not.' Some said that when people talked about Fascism they really meant Mussolini, others referred constantly to 'Mussolinismo' rather than to Fascism.

At the time Mussolini benefited from a popular belief which often helps dictators. When things went badly, people assumed that the great leader did not know about what was happening. 'If the Duce only knew…' was a common phrase, which effectively removed the fascist leader from any responsibility for the ill doings of his followers. As with Hitler, the Italian leader was thought to be above the mêlée and to be deliberately kept in the dark about problems by bad councillors, so that he was unaware of what was going on behind his back. This belief rested on the assumption, common to populist appeal, that Mussolini represented benevolent authority and that, as the son of a blacksmith, he understood the problems of ordinary Italians. His much publicized generosity in response to begging letters (there was a special fund set aside for these donations) seemed to be the guarantee

10. On the decline of the person of Mussolini in the later 1930s, see R. J. B. Bosworth, *Mussolini* (new edition), Bloomsbury, London, 2010, chs 15, 16.

of this, and it was, after all, the Duce, and not Father Christmas, who was said to bring children gifts at New Year.

Paradoxically, the more the Fascist Party was disliked, the more Mussolini seemed to be the representative of honest, paternal, authority. Like a medieval monarch, he was seen as justice fighting injustice. In fact, that phrase, invoking the intervention of the Duce—'if he only knew'—was more often than not used *against* the intemperance of fascist authority, thus pitting Mussolini against the fascists. From the evidence available it is clear that many people had created a mental distinction between the regime and the leader, living in a dual reality formed of a bad Fascism and a good *Mussolinismo*. The leader had become detached from the led—something that had obvious negative implications for the long-term future of Fascism because the more the Duce was elevated as superman, the more he became irreplaceable. Farinacci put it rather crisply when, in 1933, he warned Mussolini that too much depended on one man: 'Italy cannot have a Duce number 2'. In fact, Mussolini's birthday was not celebrated in the newspapers because it would have reminded readers of his mortality.

In a sense the cult of the Duce may even have served to weaken the regime, distracting from the thrust of the fascist totalitarian 'idea' and concentrating everything on the charisma of one person. What is certain is that the cult was beginning to break down towards the end of the 1930s (ironically, this was probably the period when Mussolini began to believe his own myth). Rumours of unsuccessful attempts on his life circulated widely in 1938 and 1939 (sometimes accompanied by expressions of regret that the attacker had not aimed better) and Mussolini's increasing absence from the public scene, particularly in the spring and summer of 1939, provoked speculation about what was said to be his rapidly declining health. But, above all, material conditions within Italy worked to deflate Mussolini's image. He had been in full control for almost two decades and there had been no improvement in the living standards of many people. In fact, by 1939, informers were reporting that things were getting worse and popular discontent increasing. Inflation, unemployment, and high taxation produced resentment and strong criticism of the regime. One Neapolitan summed up feelings succinctly: 'we work more than before, we eat less, there are shortages of everything, we're living in misery; when there wasn't all this mania for greatness we lived better and the ruling class (with rare exceptions) was exemplary in honesty and decency'.[11]

The fact was that the promised fascist utopia was still beyond the horizon, well out of sight, and popular mood reflected this. In a regime that claimed to control everything, responsibility for hardship was inevitably laid at its door and economic discontent could not but assume a political dimension. Informers' reports speak of a growing sense that the regime had lost all direction, that it was not doing its job. Uncertainty about the future was combined with discontent about the present—a dangerous mixture for a regime that had promised the earth. As already suggested in the previous chapters, the attentions of the PNF were often considered vexatious. Constant convocations to attend this meeting or that demonstration had exhausted people and, according to the reports of informers, many of those enrolled in the Party had stopped going to Party meetings or attending the local city groups. Students found the path to advancement blocked by the 'new caste' formed by the first 'fascist generation' and were only partially mollified by Bottai's reforms of 1939 which opened doors for some of them. Young people in general, more than half of whom, as studies have shown, had no particular links with the PNF,[12] were doing their best to avoid attending pre-military training and there was a diffused tendency among the majority of young people to avoid the Party whenever possible.[13] And, if they were avoiding politics, their parents were doing likewise, going to the fascist after-work club, where they spent their time drinking and playing cards—more 'alcoholized' than

11. P. Corner, *The Fascist Party and Popular Opinion in Mussolini's Italy*, Oxford, Oxford University Press, 2012, p. 235.
12. The conclusion of Dante Germino, *The Italian Fascist Party in Power. A Study in Totalitarian Rule*, Minneapolis, University of Minnesota Press, 1959.
13. It is significant that university enrolment, which exonerated students from military service, rose by almost 50% between 1939 and 1940. Even after years of indoctrination, many young people evidently had little desire to fight.

'fascistized', as one informer put it.[14] There was a widespread feeling that seventeen years of 'living dangerously' (one of Mussolini's favourite phrases) had produced few results. The Empire was a disappointment; 'we conquered the country of coffee and now we have no coffee. Let's hope we don't conquer anything else', was one comment in 1939. And there was a European war in the offing, something which, despite exposure for more than a decade to bellicose propaganda, few wanted, particularly not with Nazi Germany as an ally.[15] Apart from a general dislike of Hitler, everyone understood that an eventual German victory in a European war could only bode ill for Italy and for Italians.[16] Many saw that, win or lose in this war, Mussolini had worked his way into a corner in which he could only lose politically.

More importantly, the message was getting across that Mussolini *did* know about the corrupt state of the PNF and the shady operations of fascist officials and that he preferred to do nothing, fearing scandal; it was said that he was, in any case, now more interested in international than in national affairs. Although his reputation gained a much needed boost with Munich (but the Duce himself was irritated to be considered 'the man of peace'), there was a growing sense in the country that, with the greater dynamism of Nazi Germany very evident, Mussolini was no longer in complete control of the game. This was made abundantly clear in 1939, when it was obvious to everybody that Mussolini had not been consulted about the Molotov–Ribbentrop Pact. At that point the situation was summed up well by the stencil-graffito that appeared on walls in Rome, showing a shock of black hair, two staring eyes, and a small moustache, with written underneath 'Behold the

14. Corner, *Fascist Party*, p. 160. On the tendency in long-lasting regimes to arrive at a situation of stagnation and entropy, see R. O. Paxton, *The Anatomy of Fascism*, New York, Kopf, 2004.

15. Corner, *Fascist Party*, p. 240.

16. De Felice writes of 'depoliticization' and a 'generalized disgust with politics' among the population (see R. De Felice, *Mussolini il Duce. Gli anni del consenso 1929–36*, Turin, Einaudi, 1974, vol. 2, p. 221). On the various aspects of increasing discontent and disillusion in the population at large during the late 1930s, see Corner, *Fascist Party*, section II.

Führer, Duce of the Duce.' It was a sentiment reflected in the ironic phrase, current at the time, 'We were better off when Mussolini was in power.'

Mussolini: the memory

Nonetheless, if the cult of the Duce was subject to increasing doubt in the years immediately prior to Italy's entry into the Second World War, it seems somehow to have survived the public vilification of April 1945. Popular memory, as reflected in the commonplaces about him, is generally indulgent towards the Duce to say the least. So how is it that history and memory seem now to have become so divorced?

As we have seen, the perpetuation of the myth of Mussolini was undoubtedly aided by the circumstances of the post-war settlement, in which all Italians were cast (and cast themselves) as victims of Fascism rather than victims of Mussolini. Yet, although the politics of Fascism were discredited, the leader continued to fascinate; he still stimulated interest, even outside of his disastrous political context. As already noted, it did not take long after 1945 for newspapers and magazines to begin publishing articles on the Duce, almost always dwelling on his private, family life and emphasizing the personal aspects of the dictator. Mussolini the good family man was a persistent theme, carefully avoiding reference to the Duce's other unfortunate family. His wife, Donna Rachele—shown as a simple homespun housewife—was usually well to the fore in these reports, as were the children.[17] In many of the articles, the tone was so accommodating and free of criticism that it seemed that, had he been alive in the 1950s, Mussolini would have been the perfect Christian Democrat.

Moreover, the international context worked in favour of the image of the Duce. The onset of the Cold War made anti-communists attractive to many, and Mussolini could certainly pass muster on that

17. Bosworth, *Mussolini*, ch. 18; Baldassini, *L'ombra di Mussolini*.

score. After all, it was argued (mistakenly), what had Fascism been if not a reaction to the threat of communist revolution? With the Communist Party (PCI) a constant force in Italy until the end of the 1970s Mussolini could find his defenders without too much difficulty— at least on the Right. Giorgio Almirante and Arturo Michelini (two prominent leaders of the resurrected neo-fascist party) exploited this situation as well as they were able. And, at a more theoretical level, the fascist leader escaped without too much condemnation, with anti-communism rather than anti-Fascism becoming the dominant trope in the West. Cold War totalitarian theory spoke of Nazism and Soviet communism in the same breath but had little to say about Fascism. Indeed, Hannah Arendt excluded Italy from her discussions of totali-tarianism in her classic study; Mussolini, it seemed, was simply an authoritarian dictator and should not be considered in the same terms as Hitler and Stalin.[18] Although it took several years to make itself evident, this judgement was, of course, an invitation to Italians to employ the lesser evil argument—Mussolini was not Hitler nor Stalin—with its ready drift to rehabilitation and eventual revaluation. It was a short step from 'not as bad as' to 'did many good things'. In this process, the judgement of the man, however mistaken, tends to become, by association, a judgement of the regime.

The anti-fascist tradition has, of course, attempted consistently to keep the battle against Fascism as a constant in popular historical memory. The 25th of April (the day of liberation in 1945) remains a national holiday, although not without challenge. But, as already stated in Chapter 1, the anti-fascist tradition has tended to concentrate very heavily on the partisan struggle of the Resistance and has had little to say about the regime itself beyond reference to the few distinguished anti-fascist martyrs. The more the Resistance is celebrated as a victory over *Nazifascismo*, the more the regime itself fades into the background. That 'anti-Fascism without a Fascism' is all too evident in much of the

18. See H. Arendt, *The Origins of Totalitarianism*, New York, Harcourt, Brace and Jovanovich, 1973, p. 258 (orig. 1951).

literature. And Mussolini is not a central figure in the anti-fascist narrative of 'German' massacres of Italian civilians; his responsibility, as head of the **Repubblica sociale**, is rarely mentioned—even when he appears, he is a poor shadow of the man he was and hardly merits attention. The real Mussolini is someone else. And that Mussolini is still, in popular imagination, the man in front of the cheering crowds, the aviator, the bare-chested harvester, the dominant European states-man, the man created by the cult of the Duce.

So why are people so ready to cling to this image, patently con-structed by Fascism itself? Why is it that some are so ready to accept a carefully groomed self-representation, now passed off as historical fact? Certain of the reasons have already been identified in Chapter 1. These involve a series of factors, mostly related to the present rather than to the past. One in particular stands out. This is the desire for a sense of direction at a time of increasing uncertainty, the psycho-logical search for some kind of security in a world that seems increas-ingly insecure and in which there is a constant sense of personal impotence. In an apparent paradox, fear of the future has a lot to do with this reading of the past. Ironically Mussolini, who, as the histor-ical record shows, in his lifetime created far more insecurity than security, is identified as a person who responded to this desire for protection. The paternal aspect of dictatorship is remembered. Like Uncle Joe [Stalin], Mussolini is seen as someone who cared for his people; 'after all, he gave us pensions' is the oft-repeated theme. Above all, the Mussolini image is evoked in the current desire for someone who corresponds to the figure created by that cult—strong, sure of himself, determined, a man of justice, projected towards the future with promise and with hope. He is the winner Italy needs—a man who not only reassures at a personal level but who also responds assertively to Italy's complexes about her international reputation and ensures that other powers show Italy the respect that the nation feels to be its due. Seen in this light it is hardly surprising that the imagin-ary figure of the Duce, as created by the cult, looms large when viewed through the lens of the uncertainties of the present. Like all populists, he offers simple solutions to complex problems. An illusion about the past offers solace in the present and hope for the future.

As this book has attempted to show, this illusion needs to be destroyed. On two counts. The first is that it perpetuates that detachment of Mussolini from the regime which he inaugurated and then commanded. It creates a time-independent story, disconnected from real historical experience. It should be a banality, but it seems it is not and must be repeated: the fascist leader cannot be viewed out of context. The regime of violence, repression, corruption, and intimidation was the construction of Mussolini, the wars were the wars of Mussolini. He should be seen as responsible for all this, not as some noble figure in Palazzo Venezia preoccupied about the destiny of the Nation. To detach the man from his context is to perpetuate the idea that 'Mussolini didn't know'. This idea has to be laid to rest and this can only be done by refreshing our knowledge of the workings of the regime itself and of the Duce's position at the centre of that regime. Furthermore, the excessive concentration on the person of the Duce impedes a real appreciation of what the regime represented. It permits us to forget the system based on intolerance, repression of dissent, and even murder.

But the second reason is perhaps more telling and it has to do with precisely this currently distorted image of the fascist leader. The plain fact is that the nostalgics have got the wrong man. Mussolini was, in reality, very far from being that strong, decided, far-sighted figure imagined by those indulgent towards the Duce. He was not the fantasized strong leader. He was, in many respects, a weak dictator, ultimately able to control only a part of what was going on around him.[19] In moments of coquetry, Mussolini would himself observe that the American president, Franklin Roosevelt, had more power than he had, which, if not accurate, nonetheless reflected a recognition of limits.

19. R. J. B. Bosworth, 'Dictators strong or weak? The model of Benito Mussolini', in R. J. B. Bosworth (ed.), *The Oxford Handbook of Fascism*, Oxford, Oxford University Press, 2010.

Mussolini's weakness derived fundamentally from the fact that he knew that Fascism could go so far and only so far in respect of existing centres of power within the country, that the fascist victory was only a partial victory and that it could never be complete. The monarchy was, of course, the first hindrance to absolute rule, the Church the second; others included the armed forces, the important industrial and agrarian interests, and state bureaucracy. Mussolini—certainly a very astute politician—was able to manoeuvre around problems, make agreements, appease those with vested interests, arrive at compromises, all of which ensured his personal position, but he knew full well that any kind of move towards a fully intransigent Fascism—a regime with a fascist in every position of power and a blackshirt behind every desk—would have generated an opposition in the country that he was in no position to counter. Fascist control, based on what has been called the 'authoritarian compromise' with existing centres of power, could never be absolute.[20]

Awareness of the limits of fascist power explains why the fascist leader marginalized the more hot-headed fascists when they began to push for the second wave of the 'revolution' following the murder of Matteotti; it explains why he was very careful to keep the radical fascist Roberto Farinacci on the sidelines, and it was for this same reason that he preferred to make the prefect rather than the local Party boss the most important figure in provincial politics. The prefect answered to the Ministry of the Interior—that is, to the state—not to the Fascist Party. By remaining anchored to the state (and, as 1943 was to show to his cost, to the monarchy) rather than to the Party, Mussolini avoided having to follow his many more radical but less realistic colleagues in a battle he (and they) had little hope of winning.

Mussolini was essentially a mediator between interest groups and centres of power, often using one against the other, often compromising

---

20. M. Legnani, 'Sistema di potere fascista, blocco dominante, alleanze sociali', in A. Del Boca, M. Legnani, and M. G. Rossi (eds), *Il regime fascista. Storia e storiografia*, Rome-Bari, Laterza, 1995.

with non-fascist interests in order to defend and increase his own personal power, but suffering nonetheless from the fact that all too often it seemed that everyone had their own view of what Fascism meant. He never enjoyed the authority of Hitler, who could in any case rely on the SS to bring almost anyone into line (the fascist MVSN never fulfilled the same function) and, who, after 1934, had no institutional barriers to his exercise of power. But even recognizing the constraints within which Mussolini operated, there is considerable evidence, from archives, memoirs, and diplomatic reports, that the fascist leader insisted on being consulted about everything, read and commented on vast quantities of documents (unlike Hitler), but was actually bad at making decisions. He relied on intuition, liked to make an impression with his impromptu 'decisiveness', and, in later years, was accused of making choices on the basis of the advice of the last person he had talked to, often changing his position in the course of a morning. Guido Leto, head of OVRA for many years, recorded how Mussolini would approve proposals that were 'diametrically' opposed to each other, creating conflicts in the administration,[21] and, in the later years, Giuseppe Bottai frequently found Mussolini uncertain, unhappy, and confused. This was hands-on politics in uncertain hands; a firm, secure hand, inspiring confidence of judgement, was not very apparent.

None of this should detract from the seriousness of the totalitarian project. The problems lay in putting that project into effect, and here the regime showed its weaknesses. In the years immediately before Italy's entry into the Second World War the overall impression of the workings of the fascist state is that of confusion, with many—too many—initiatives proposed but almost none followed through to any kind of successful conclusion. As we have seen with the *parastato*, immense bureaucratic expansion often produced paralysis. There is little evidence that the so-called 'totalitarian phase' of Fascism after 1936—a phase intended to infuse a new dynamism into a stagnating

---

21. Guido Leto, quoted in A. Aquarone, *L'organizzazione dello stato totalitario*, Turin, Einaudi, 1965 (1995), p. 305.

movement, a phase intended to re-state Italy's fascist superiority in respect of Nazi Germany—shifted the Party from a concentration on activities judged by many fascists to be routine, concerned only with *esteriorità*—that is, all show and no content.[22] What one senses is a kind of drift caused by an uncertainty of ultimate objectives. Precisely what Mussolini's plan for the future was remained unclear, changing often from one day to the next in his fantasy schemes for an Italian control of *Mare nostrum* and the whole Mediterranean area.

In some ways this lack of clarity was built into the situation, it was structural, because the contradictions of the fascist compromise could not be reconciled. Efforts at radicalization of the movement were inevitably going to provoke conflict with those conservative forces who had always been among the strongest supporters of the regime. For this reason a renewed dynamism, required by the second half of the 1930s, was likely to create as many problems as it solved. Mussolini does not seem to have been able to confront this dilemma. More interested in crowds than in people, he was a bad judge of collaborators. The replacement in 1939 of Achille Starace as Party secretary, first by the former blackshirt hero Ettore Muti and then by the efficient (and very fascist) Adelchi Serena was an attempt to revive the Party, but Serena's rapid replacement by the extremely young (and very useless) Aldo Vidussoni was an index of Mussolini's uncertainty. Serena was too radical and had to go; his successor was totally anodyne and could not even get near to rescuing the Party from its atrophy. Getting the right person for the job was not easy when it was not clear what the job was. Unlike Hitler, who had the German nation 'working towards the Führer' and could sit back and let others do the work, Mussolini found that, despite his personal power, his position as

---

22. The lack of dynamism was evinced at a seminar in Rome in the 1990s when Vittorio Foà—anti-fascist, politician, and trade union leader—famously summed up the last years of the regime with one word, 'Boredom'. (His elder sister immediately put him in his place with the observation, 'What do you know about it? You were always in prison.')

dictator of a regime of fragmented interests and diverse ambitions posed problems he was unable to resolve.

The idea that Mussolini was the strong leader who could solve everything is based on illusion—an illusion now masquerading as memory. It is a 'memory' formed from a lengthy process of selection of what to remember and what to forget—a process begun immediately after the death of the Duce and continued through the following years. As is obvious, memory, even collective memory, is necessarily subjective, but that subjectivity is conditioned by and responds to what it encounters—what we might call the social inputs to memory. In cases already cited elsewhere in this book the process is not difficult to understand. Former Soviet citizens (and the generations now following them) have constructed a collective memory around a negative comparison between communist past and market-driven present; former East Germans have, in the same way, formed a memory of the GDR that is built around inputs based on what seems to them to be a subordination of the territories of the former Democratic Republic to the interests of the Federal Republic. What this book has attempted to do is to suggest that, in Italy, the inputs to collective memory seem to have been severely manipulated over the years, that they correspond more to what many would like to believe than to the realities of the regime, and that the process of 'remembering' has involved suppression of much and distortion of a great deal that remains. As a consequence, this 'memory', at least at a popular level, is often a construct based more on non-historical than on historical factors.

In effect, at least in Italy, this 'memory-forming' selection has been a complex operation because it has involved, certainly, the construction of a partial vision of the past but it has also had a lot to do with the present. If history is a critical discourse based on the elaboration of evidence, memory is much more related to self-image. Thus the 'memory' of the fascist period touches the troubled and sensitive contemporary question of Italian identity. The credit conceded to Mussolini is, in the final analysis, not only about the Duce, it is also about the self-image of Italians, about an unwillingness on the part of some to assume any kind of even partial responsibility for involvement in a past heavy with some of the greatest tragedies of the twentieth century. Just as the 'consensus' thesis has been interpreted in such a way as to provide self-absolution, the plea of the 'one mistake' is used to sweep responsibilities under the carpet and is, by implication, a vindication of all the other aspects of the regime. Thus vindicated, responsibility for Fascism ceases to be an issue—because Fascism was not so bad; thus, coming to terms with the past is for others, not for us. Collective memory responds to this kind of input.

It should be clear that it is not a question of settling old scores or of pronouncing a simplistic moral condemnation. Any treatment of Fascism has to tread the difficult path between a ritualistic moral condemnation on the one side and, on the other, the resort to a historicism of the regime which makes it fade, innocuous and without distinguishing features, into a more general European past. The dangers of both are evident. The first, without the backing of detailed historical research, is always just an opinion and stops short of helping historical understanding; the second fails to identify those key aspects which distinguish the regime from other historical moments and reduces Fascism to an unexceptional period within a continuous Italian history. What is at issue here is the formation of a realistic memory of the past that also works in the present. This kind of memory should permit a better understanding of continuities and discontinuities with the fascist past, thus helping to clarify how Italy has related to the world about it, both in the past and in the present. All of which would help us towards a better comprehension of what Italian identity actually means. That this is part of a larger problem concerning the way Italy positions itself in the contemporary world is evident, but it is equally clear that a firm and realistic assessment of the past is one of the best ways of forming a convinced and convincing national identity. True, history as such is not enough to form national identity, which has many components, but identity based on avoiding the past, on reliance on myth and illusion, is at best uncertain. In particular, the illusion that Fascism was essentially innocuous and Mussolini an efficient and benevolent leader cannot be considered mistaken but essentially harmless; it is an illusion that is damaging because of the way in which it speaks to the present.

Like other twentieth-century dictators, Mussolini presided over a regime that was corrupt, inefficient, and, at times, brutal, but which presented, and communicated, a very positive face to the outside world. Fascism constructed its own 'phantom utopia' during the *ventennio*—a utopia that, like its Soviet and German counterparts, made constant reference to a radiant future, nowhere more in evidence than in the propaganda posters of the time in which the sun is always shining on the horizon. People were invited to live in both the difficult present and the promised future utopia; the dual reality present in all totalitarianisms was present in Italy as well. And, as we know, utopia, precisely because it is a fantasy related to the future, has the habit of resisting the passage of time. Yet this utopian gloss should not be allowed to continue to obscure the negative reality. In the case of Italy, what were undoubtedly the seemingly attractive aspects of the regime linked to this utopian dream—security, order, international dignity and prowess—have remained tantalizingly out of reach in many more recent moments when confidence in the state has sometimes arrived at a very low ebb and Italy has appeared impotent on the international stage. The fascist message—'we are the best and the world will be forced to recognize this'—still carries weight in a country persistently questioning its role and its identity. Small wonder, therefore, that we find elements of the fascist dream now confusingly entangled with the realities of the regime to the extent that they begin to dominate in the collective memory. The promises and the hopes begin to obliterate the hardships, the privations, the regimentation—and the hundreds of thousands of graves.

The irony of this edulcorated 'memory' is that it conflicts diametrically with the assessment of the achievements of the regime by the person who was perhaps best able to assess those achievements—Mussolini himself. In 1943 Mussolini would refer to 'the indigestions of totalitarianism', meaning the great difficulty of getting all the components of a polycentric would-be totalitarian regime to work together, the difficulty of getting all the cogs to mesh in such a way as to form a 'total' system. Reflecting on the many incompatible impulses that had emerged as the regime progressed, he listed 'Government, Party, Monarchy, Army, Militia, prefects, local bosses, the chiefs of the Confederations [of Industry, Agriculture] and the enormous interests of the monopoly-holders'.[23] Getting them all to collaborate had been beyond him. He would also speak of the problems of trying to rule 'this very great, very small, Italian people'[24]—'not so much difficult as pointless' is the phrase often attributed to him—again indicating that something had not worked as it should. Almost inevitably he blamed others for his failure—the bourgeoisie, the Party, his fawning and cor-rupt advisers, the Italians in general (of whom he voiced increasing scorn). This recognition of failure, related in the main (as can be seen from his long list of culprits) not to the immediate circumstances of the war itself but to long-term, structural factors, corresponds little to the image of the triumphant Duce that inhabits present-day popular memory—a 'memory' that prefers the legend to the reality. The reality is that the man whose political platform had been the resolution of what he considered to be the problems of the Italian nation—the feuds generated by party politics, the divisiveness of region and class, the tensions between public and private interest, a perceived lack of international respect for Italy—succeeded only in exacerbating those problems through the creation of a fragile, unstable, and corrupt populist-authoritarian system that, in the end, satisfied few and alien-ated an ever-increasing number.

We began this book by observing the ways in which nostalgia for past authoritarian regimes may contribute to paving the way for a

23. O. Dinale, *Quarant'anni di colloqui con lui*, Milan, Ciarocca, 1953, p. 181, cit. in Aquarone, *Organizzazione*, p. 302.
24. Ibid.

new authoritarianism. Our current situation is that, while communism (at least in its classic form) has disappeared with surprising speed
from the political arena, we are talking once again about Fascism.
Certainly, the dangers of a new Fascism probably come from a largely
uncharted, possibly digital, direction, and we should not spend too
much time listening for the sound of the jackboots. But, from whatever direction they come, these dangers should not be buttressed by
illusions about the past which put myth before reality. Historically,
there can be few doubts that Italian Fascism was a failure—a very
costly failure. This suggests that those who are still indulgent towards
Fascism and enthralled by the myth of the Duce should open their
eyes and look a little more closely at the realities that lie hidden behind
that myth. Their 'memory' may be deceiving them. If they look hard
and reflect a little, they may even discover that much of what they
think about Mussolini, much of what they 'remember' about Mussolini,
is not really about Mussolini at all.

Select bibliography

Although not exclusively, this Bibliography has been compiled with an eye to works available in English. Other titles, including many available only in Italian, can be found in the notes.

Albanese, G. *The March on Rome. Violence and the Rise of Italian Fascism*, London, Routledge, 2019

Albanese, G., and Pergher, R. (eds), *In the Society of Fascists. Acclamation, Acquiescence, and Agency in Mussolini's Italy*, New York, Palgrave Macmillan, 2012

Alexievich, S. *Secondhand Time. The Last of the Soviets*, New York, Random House, 2016 (orig. Russian 2013)

Aquarone, A. *L'organizzazione dello stato totalitario*, Turin, Einaudi, 1965 (1995)

Aquarone, A. 'Violenza e consenso nel Fascismo italiano', *Storia contemporanea*, I, 1979

Arthurs, J., Ebner, M., and Ferris, K. (eds). *The Politics of Everyday Life in Fascist Italy. Outside the State?*, New York, Palgrave Macmillan, 2017

Balbo, I. *Diario 1922*, Milan, Mondadori, 1932

Baldassini, C. 'Fascismo e memoria. L'autorappresentazione dello squadrismo', *Contemporanea*, 5, July 2002

Battini, M. *The Missing Italian Nuremberg. Cultural Amnesia and Postwar Politics*, Basingstoke, Palgrave Macmillan, 2007

Benedusi, L. *The Enemy of the New Man. Homosexuality in Fascist Italy*, Madison, University of Wisconsin Press, 2012

Ben Ghiat, R. *Fascist Modernities. Italy 1922–1945*, Berkeley and Los Angeles, University of California Press, 2001

Ben Ghiat, R. 'A lesser evil? Italian Fascism in/and the totalitarian equation', in H. Dubiel and G. Motzkin (eds), *The Lesser Evil. Moral Approaches to Genocide Practices*, New York, Routledge, 2004

Bosworth, R. J. B. *Mussolini*, Oxford, Oxford University Press, 2002

Bosworth, R. J. B. 'Everyday Mussolinismo. Friends, family, locality, and violence in Fascist Italy', *Contemporary European History*, 14, 2005

Bosworth, R. J. B. *Mussolini's Italy. Life under the Dictatorship, 1915–1945*, London, Penguin, 2006

Bosworth, R. J. B. 'Dictators strong or weak? The model of Benito Mussolini', *The Oxford Handbook of Fascism*, Oxford, Oxford University Press, 2010

Bosworth, R. J. B. *Claretta. Mussolini's Last Lover*, New Haven, Yale University Press, 2017

Bottai, G. *Vent'anni e un giorno*, Milan, 1949 (new edition, Milan, Rizzoli, 2008)

Canali, M. *Le spie del regime*, Bologna, Il Mulino, 2004

Canali, M. 'The Matteotti murder and the origins of Mussolini's totalitarian Fascist regime in Italy', *Journal of Modern Italian Studies*, 2, 2009

Cannistraro, P. V. *La fabbrica del consenso. Fascismo e mass-media*, Rome-Bari, Laterza 1974

Cardoza, A. L. *Agrarian Elites and Italian Fascism. The Province of Bologna 1901–1926*, Princeton, Princeton University Press, 1982

Cardoza, A. L. *Mussolini. The First Fascist*, London, Longman, 2005

Cassese, S. *Lo stato fascista*, Bologna, Il Mulino, 2010

Ciocca, P. L. *Ricchi per sempre? Una storia economica d'Italia*, Turin, Bollati Boringhieri, 2007

Clark, M. *Mussolini. A Study in Power*, London, Pearson Longman, 2005

Confino, A. 'Collective memory and cultural history. Problems of method', *American Historical Review*, 102, 5, December 1997

Cooke, P. *The Legacy of the Italian Resistance*, New York, Palgrave Macmillan, 2011

Corner, P. *Fascism in Ferrara 1915–1925*, London, Oxford University Press, 1975

Corner, P. 'Italian Fascism. Whatever happened to dictatorship?', *Journal of Modern History*, 74 (2002)

Corner, P. (ed.). *Popular Opinion in Totalitarian Regimes. Fascism, Nazism, Communism*, Oxford, Oxford University Press, 2009

Corner, P. 'Italian Fascism. Organization, enthusiasm, opinion', *Journal of Modern Italian Studies*, 15, 2010

Corner, P. *The Fascist Party and Popular Opinion in Mussolini's Italy*, Oxford, Oxford University Press, 2012

Corner, P. 'Dictatorship revisited. Consensus, coercion, and strategies of survival', *Modern Italy*, 4, 2017

Corner, P. (with Lim Jie-Hyun). *The Palgrave Handbook of Mass Dictatorship*, Basingstoke, Palgrave Macmillan, 2016

De Felice, R. *Mussolini*, 7 vols, Turin, Einaudi, 1966–97; vol. 3.1, *Mussolini il Duce. Gli anni del consenso 1929–36*, Turin, Einaudi, 1974; vol. 3.2, *Lo Stato totalitario 1936–1940*, Turin, Einaudi, 1981

De Grazia, V. *The Culture of Consent. Mass Organisation of Leisure in Fascist Italy*, Cambridge, Cambridge University Press, 1981

De Grazia, V. *How Fascism Ruled Women. Italy 1922–45*, Berkeley, University of California Press, 1993

De Grazia, V. *Irresistible Empire*, Cambridge, Mass., Harvard University Press, 2005

Dogliani, P. *Il Fascismo degli italiani. Una storia sociale*, Turin, UTET, 2008 (reprint, with updated bibliography, 2014)

Duggan, C. *Fascist Voices. An Intimate History of Mussolini's Italy*, London, Bodley Head, 2013

Duggan, C., Gundle, S., and Pieri, G. (eds). *The Cult of the Duce. Mussolini and the Italians*, Manchester, Manchester University Press, 2013

Dunnage, J. *The Italian Police and the Rise of Fascism. A Case Study of the Province of Bologna, 1897–1925*, Westport, Conn., Praeger, 1997

Dunnage, J. 'Surveillance and denunciation in fascist Siena, 1927–1943', *English Historical Quarterly*, 28, 2, 2008

Dunnage, J. 'Ideology, clientelism and the "fascistisation" of the Italian state. Fascists in the Interior Ministry Police', *Journal of Modern Italian Studies*, 3, 2009

Duranti, S. *Lo spirito gregario*, Rome, Donzelli, 2008

Ebner, M. 'The political police and denunciation during Fascism. A review of recent historical literature', *Journal of Modern Italian Studies*, 11, 2, 2006

Ebner, M. *Ordinary Violence in Mussolini's Italy*, Cambridge, Cambridge University Press, 2011

Ellwood, D. W. *Italy 1943–45. The Politics of Liberation*, Leicester, Leicester University Press, 1985

Ellwood, D. W. *The Shock of America. Europe and the Challenge of the Century*, Oxford, Oxford University Press, 2012

Fabbri, F. *Le origini della guerra civile. L'Italia dalla Grande Guerra al Fascismo, 1918–1921*, Milan, UTET, 2010

Ferris, K. *Everyday Life in Fascist Venice*, London, Palgrave Macmillan, 2012

Filippi, F. *Mussolini ha fatto anche cose buone*, Turin, Bollati Boringhieri, 2018

Finaldi, G. 'Fascism, violence, and Italian colonialism', *Journal of Holocaust Research*, 33, 1, 2019

Finkelstein, F. *Transatlantic Fascism. Ideology, Violence, and the Sacred in Argentina and Italy 1919–1945*, Durham, NC, Duke University Press, 2010

Fitzpatrick, S. 'Russia under pre-war Stalinism', in Corner (ed.), *Popular Opinion in Totalitarian Regimes. Fascism, Nazism, Communism*, Oxford, Oxford University Press, 2009

Focardi, F. 'La memoria della guerra e il mito del "bravo italiano". Origine e affermazione di un autoritratto collettivo', *Italia contemporanea*, September–December 2000

Focardi, F. *La guerra della memoria. La Resistenza nel dibattito politico dal 1945 ad oggi*, Rome-Bari, Laterza, 2006

Focardi, F. *Il cattivo tedesco e il bravo italiano. La rimozione delle colpe della seconda guerra mondiale* (3rd edn), Rome–Bari, Laterza, 2016

Focardi, F. *Nel cantiere della memoria. Fascismo. Resistenza, Shoah, Foibe*, Rome, Viella, 2020

Franzinelli, M. *I tentacoli dell'OVRA. Agenti, collaboratori e vittimi cella polizia politica fascista*, Turin, Bollati Boringhieri, 1999

Franzinelli, M. *Squadristi! Protagonisti e techniche della violenza fascista 1919–1922*, Milan, Mondadori, 2004

Frei, N. 'Hitler's popular support', in Hans Mommsen (ed.), *The Third Reich between Vision and Reality. New Perspectives on German History*, Oxford, Berg, 1991

Gentile, E. *Il culto del littorio*, Rome–Bari, Laterza, 1993

Gentile, E. *Storia del Partito Fascista 1919–1922. Movimento e milizia*, Rome–Bari, Laterza, 1989

Gentile, E. *Le origini dell'ideologia fascista*, Bologna, Il Mulino, 1996 (1st edn 1975)

Germino, D. *The Italian Fascist Party in Power. A Study in Totalitarian Rule*, Minneapolis, University of Minneapolis Press, 1959

Gessen, M. *The Future is History. How Totalitarianism Reclaimed Russia*, New York, Riverhead, 2017

Giorgi, C. *La previdenza del regime. Storia dell'Inps durante il Fascismo*. Bologna, Il Mulino, 2004

Giorgi, C., and Pavan, I. *Storia dello Stato sociale in Italia*, Bologna, Il Mulino, 2020

Goeschel, C. *Mussolini and Hitler. The Forging of the Fascist Alliance*, New Haven, Yale University Press, 2018

Gooch, J. *Mussolini's War. Fascist Italy from Triumph to Collapse (1935–43)*, London, Penguin, 2020

Gregor, A. J. *Fascism as Developmental Dictatorship*, Princeton, Princeton University Press, 1979

Griffin, R. *The Nature of Fascism*, London, Pinter, 1991

Griffin, R. (ed.). *Fascism*, Oxford, Oxford University Press, 1995

Griffin, R. *Modernism and Fascism. The Sense of a New Beginning under Mussolini and Hitler*, Basingstoke, Palgrave Macmillan, 2007

Gundle, S. *Mussolini's Dream Factory. Film Stardom in Fascist Italy*, New York, Berghahn Books, 2013

Halberstam, M. *Totalitarianism and the Modern Conception of Politics*, New Haven, Yale University Press, 1999

Ipsen, C. *Dictating Demography. The Problem of Population in Fascist Italy*, Cambridge, Cambridge University Press, 1996

Judt, T. 'The past is another country. Myth and memory in postwar Europe', in I. Deak, J. T. Gross, and T. Judt (eds), *The Politics of Retribution in Europe. World War II and its Aftermath*, Princeton, Princeton University Press, 2000

Kershaw, I. *Popular Opinion and Political Dissent in the Third Reich. Bavaria 1933–1945*, Oxford, Clarendon Press, 1983

Kershaw, I. *The 'Hitler Myth'. Image and Reality in the Third Reich*, Oxford, Oxford University Press, 1987

Kershaw, I. *Hitler, 1889–1936. Hubris*, London, Penguin, 1998

Kershaw, I. *Hitler. 1936–1945. Nemesis*, London, Penguin, 2000

Kershaw, I. *Hitler, the Jews, and the Final Solution*, Jerusalem, Yad Vashem, 2008

Lee, N. 'The theory of mass dictatorship. A re-examination of the Park Chung Hee period', *Review of Korean Studies*, 12, 3, September 2009

Lim, J.-H. 'Historical perspectives of "mass dictatorship"', *Totalitarian Movements and Political Religions*, 6, 3, 2005

Lüdtke, A. *The History of Everyday Life. Reconstructing Historical Experience and Ways of Life*, Princeton, Princeton University Press, 1995

Lüdtke, A. (ed.). *Everyday Life in Mass Dictatorship. Collusion and Evasion*, Basingstoke, Palgrave Macmillan, 2017

Lupo, S. *L'utopia totalitaria del Fascismo 1918–1942*, in M. Aymard and G. Giarrizzo (eds), *Storia dell' Italia. Le regioni dall' Unità ad oggi*, Turin, Einaudi 1997

Lupo, S. *Il Fascismo. La politica di un regime totalitario*, Rome, Donzelli, 2000

Lyttelton, A. 'Fascism in Italy. The second wave', *Journal of Contemporary Italian History*, 1, 1966

Lyttelton, A. *The Seizure of Power. Fascism in Italy, 1919–1929*, London, Weidenfeld and Nicholson, 1973 (3rd edn 2004)

Lyttelton, A. 'Cause e caratteristiche della violenza fascista. Fattori costanti e fattori congiunturali', in L. Casali (ed.), *Bologna 1920. Le origini del Fascismo*, Bologna, Cappelli, 1982

Lyttelton, A. 'Fascismo e violenza. Conflitti sociale e azione politica in Italia del primo dopoguerra', *Storia contemporanea*, 6, 1982

Lyttelton, A. (ed.). *Liberal and Fascist Italy*, Oxford, Oxford University Press, 2002

Mack Smith, D. *Mussolini's Roman Empire*, London, Penguin, 1977

Melis, G. *Storia dell'amministrazione italiana*, Bologna, Il Mulino, 1996

Melis, G. (ed.). *Lo Stato negli anni trenta. Istituzioni e regimi fascisti in Europa*, Bologna, Il Mulino, 2008

Melis, G. *La macchina imperfetta. Immagini e realtà dello Stato fascista*, Bologna, Il Mulino, 2019

Millan, M. 'The institutionalisation of "squadrismo". Disciplining paramilitary violence in the Italian fascist dictatorship', *Contemporary European History*, 22, 4, 2013

Millan, M. *Squadrismo e squadristi nella dittatura fascista*, Rome, Viella, 2014

Morgan, P. 'The Party is everywhere'. The Italian fascist party in economic life, 1926–40', *English Historical Review*, 114, February 1999

Morgan, P. 'The prefects and party–state relations in fascist Italy', *Journal of Modern Italian Studies*, 3, 3, 1998

Morgan, P. *Fascism in Europe*, London, Routledge, 2003

Morgan, P. *Italian Fascism, 1915–1945* (2nd edn), Basingstoke, Palgrave Macmillan, 2004

Morris, J. *The Political Economy of Shopkeeping in Milan, 1886–1922*, Cambridge, Cambridge University Press, 1993

Musiedlak, D. *Lo stato fascista e la sua classe politica 1922–1943*, Bologna, Il Mulino, 2003

Mussolini, B. *Opera omnia*, 44 vols, ed. E. Susmel and D. Susmel, Florence, La Fenice, 1951–63, Rome, Volpe, 1978–80

Overy, R. *The Dictators*, London, Allen Lane, 2004

Padulo, G. *L'ingrata progenie. Grande guerra, massoneria, e origini del Fascismo (1914–23)*, Siena, Nuova Immagini, 2018

Palla, M., and Giovannini, P. (eds). *Il Fascismo dalle mani sporche. Dittatura, corruzione, affarismo*, Rome-Bari, Laterza, 2019

Paxton, R. O. *The Anatomy of Fascism*, New York, Knopf, 2004

Pellizzi, C. *Una rivoluzione mancata*, Milan, 1949 (new edn Bologna, Il Mulino, 2009)

Petersen, J. 'Il problema della violenza nel Fascismo italiano', *Storia contemporanea*, 6, 1982

Piazzesi, M. *Diario di uno squadrista toscano 1919–1922*, Rome, Bonacci, 1980

Pisanty, V. *I guardiani della memoria e il ritorno della destra xenofoba*, Milan, Bompiani, 2019

Preston, P. *The Spanish Holocaust. Inquisition and Extermination in Twentieth-Century Spain*, London, Harper, 2011

Procacci, Giovanna. 'La società come una caserma. La svolta repressiva nell'Italia della grande guerra', *Contemporanea*, 3, 2006

Procacci, Giovanna. *Warfare-welfare. Intervento dello Stato e diritti dei cittadini (1914–18)*, Rome, Carocci, 2013

Procacci, Giovanna. 'Il fronte interno prima e dopo Caporetto. Il fascio di difesa parlamentare', in P. G. Zunino (ed.), *Caporetto 1917. Un passo dalla 'finis Italiae'?*, Bologna, Il Mulino, 2020

Quine, M. S. *Italy's Social Revolution. Charity and Welfare from Liberalism to Fascism*, New York, Palgrave Macmillan, 2002

Reichardt, S. *Faschistiche Kampfbünde. Gewalt und Gemeinschaft im italienischen Squadrismus und der deutschen SA*, Böhlau, 2002 (Italian trans. *Camicie nere, camicie brune. Milizie fasciste in Italia e in Germania*, Bologna, Il Mulino, 2009)

Rochat, G. *Italo Balbo*, Turin, UTET, 1986

Salvati, M. *Il regime e gli impiegati. La nazionalizzazione piccolo-borghese nel ventennio fascista*, Rome-Bari, Laterza 1992

Salvati, M. *L'inutile salotto. L'abitazione piccolo-borghese nell'Italia fascista*, Turin, Bollati Boringhieri, 1993

Salvati, M. 'The long history of corporativism in Italy. A question of culture or economics?', *Contemporary European History*, 15, 2, May 2006

Santomassimo, G. *La terza via fascista. Il mito del corporativismo*, Bologna, Il Mulino, 2006

Sarfatti, M. *The Jews in Mussolini's Italy from Equality to Persecution*, Madison, University of Wisconsin Press, 2006

Schmidt, C. *The Plough and the Sword*, New York, Columbia University Press, 1938

Sierp, A. *History, Memory, and Trans-European Identity. Unifying Divisions*, London, Routledge, 2014

Stephenson, J. 'Popular opinion in Nazi Germany. Mobilization, experience, perceptions. The view from the Wurttemberg countryside', in Corner (ed.), *Popular Opinion in Totalitarian Regimes. Fascism, Nazism, Communism*, Oxford, Oxford University Press, 2009

Suzzi Valli, R. 'The myth of squadrismo in the fascist regime', *Journal of Contemporary History*, 35, 2, April 2000

Tabor, D. 'Operai in camicia nera? La composizione operaia del *fascio* di Torino, 1921–1931', *Storia e problemi contemporanei*, 36, 2004

Toniolo, G. (ed.), *Lo sviluppo economico italiano 1861–1940*, Rome-Bari, Laterza 1973

Tooze, A. *The Wages of Destruction. The Making and Breaking of the Nazi Economy*, New York, Viking, 2006

Ventura, A. *Italia ribelle. Sommosse popolari e rivolte militari nel 1920*, Rome, Carocci, 2021

Vinci, A. M. *Sentinelle della patria. Il Fascismo al confine orientale 1918–1941*, Rome-Bari, Laterza, 2011

Vivarelli, R. *Storia delle origini del Fascismo. L'Italia dall grande guerra alla marcia su Roma*, Bologna, Il Mulino, 1991–2012

Willson, P. *Peasant Women and Politics in Fascist Italy. The Massaie rurali*, London, Routledge, 2002

Willson, P. 'Italian Fascism and the political mobilisation of working-class women 1937–43', *Contemporary European History*, 22, 2013

Woller, H. *I conti con il Fascismo. L'epurazione in Italia 1943–48*, Bologna, Il Mulino, 1997

Yurchak, A. *Everything was Forever, until it Was no More. The Last Soviet Generation*, Princeton, Princeton University Press, 2005

Zuccotti, S. *The Italians and the Holocaust. Persecution, Rescue, and Survival*, Lincoln, University of Nebraska Press, 1987

Index

For the benefit of digital users, indexed terms that span two pages (e.g., 52–53) may, on occasion, appear on only one of those pages.

dictatorships
  'coerced consensus' 54
  collective enterprise, as 143
  comeback in public perceptions 2–3
  consensus and repression in
    relation 50
  contextualized approach to 6
  corruption 1–2, 97–8
  'developmental dictatorship' 128
  illusion of efficiency 127–8
  longevity 16–17
  mass mobilization 143
  nostalgia 63, 144
  paternalism 155–6
  popular participation 143
  reliance on repression 16–17
  resource allocation 85–6
  top-down perspective 20–1
diplomacy *see* international relations
dissent *see* resistance
domination *see* control
Duce *see* personality cult

economic development *see*
  modernization
empire *see* imperialism
enthusiasm *see* consent

facts *see* truth
family policy *see* society
Fascism
  anti-communism 46–7
  anti-Fascism without Fascism 13–15,
    17–18, 20
  author's approach 5–6, 19, 21–2
  capitalism and *see* capitalism
  class system, and *see* class system;
    middle class; working class
  Cold War anti-communist
    rehabilitation of 154
  corruption *see* corruption
  future, vision of *see* future
  future of Mussolini's personality
    cult and 150
  'good-natured' Fascism, myth of 6–8,
    27–8, 37–8
  Italian people as victims 13, 16–17
  'many good things'
    perspective 11–12
  'mass consensus' for 15–16

  memory of *see* memory
  modernization and *see* modernization
  moral analysis of 17–18
  Mussolini-centred view of 18–20
  mythology *see* mythology
  neglect in histories of
    totalitarianism 5–6, 13–14
  neo-Fascism distinguished 7–8
  new Fascism, current rise of 6
  'normalization' of 11–12
  re-acquisition into Italian history
    21–2
  reasons for rehabilitation of 19–20
  rehabilitation 6–8
  resistance to *see* resistance
  right-wing rehabilitation of
    18–19
  system of domination, as 21–2
  violence *see* violence
  see also *squadrismo*
Fascist Party
  current re-incarnation of 154
  dislike of elections 69
  local organization 39, 52–3, 60,
    132–3, 157
  police and 40–1, 52–3
  popularity of, compared with
    Mussolini 150
  prefects and 157
  rallies 52–3
  role of 44
  state administrative agencies,
    and 132–3
fascists
  post-War demonization 13
  post-War rehabilitation 13–14
  see also blackshirts
film industry, films *see* cinema
foreign relations *see* international
  relations
freedoms *see* rights
future
  'developmental dictatorship', and 128
  Fascism, of 150
  fascist vision of 18–19, 75–6, 130,
    133–4, 147–8, 155–6, 158–9, 162
  fear of 151–2, 155–6
  hope for 4, 10, 147–8, 155–6, 162
  imperialist vision of 112–13
  militarist vision of 121

personality cult
  breakdown of 150–1
  creation of 144, 146–7
  cultural construct, as 148–9
  current popular imagination, in 154–6
  disillusionment with fascist regime,
    and 151–3
  effectiveness 148–9
  emphasis and exaggeration 146–7
  Fascist Party popularity, and 150–1
  imperialism and 147–8
  importance 147
  memory of Mussolini, and 144
  modernization and 130–1
  Mussolini's early example 146
  physicality 148
  popular belief 149
  power and 144
  propaganda and 64–5, 144, 147
  vision of the future 148, 150, 155–6
  zenith 147
perspective see memory
politics
  exclusion of political rights 70–1
  left-wing appropriation of anti-fascist
    'myth' 16–17
  memory and political
    expediency 13–14
  official memory 15
  reasons for rehabilitation of
    Fascism 19–20
  revisionist history, and 16–17
  right-wing rehabilitation of
    Mussolini 18–19
Pontine marshes see propaganda
popular opinion see consent; resistance
power
  corruption and 1–2
  see also control
propaganda
  anti-Semitism, and 115–16
  cinema 52–3
  control and 68–9
  family policy, and 92–3
  fascist vision of the future, and 162
  imperialism and 110
  mafia eradication, and 98–9
  modernization, and 23–4, 134–6
  personality cult, and 64–5, 144, 147
  Pontine marshes reclamation 134–7
  present-day persistence of 65

Second World War 151–2
  social policy, and 70–1
  welfare system, and 85
  see also cinema
psychology see memory

rehabilitation see history, historiography
religion and state see Catholic Church
repression see control
resistance
  anti-fascist tradition, and 103–4, 154–5
  blacklisting against 13
  blackmail against 54–5
  distorted memory of 13
  German occupation, to 102–3
  imperialism, to 107
revisionist history see history,
  historiography
rights
  demand for 70–1
  denial and repression of 1–2
  employers' rights 71–2
  exclusion of political rights 70–1, 82–3
  fascist ideology, in 70–1, 82–3
  labour rights 71–2
  property 79–80
  realization of 30–1
  welfare rights 83–4
right-wing see politics
Roman Catholic Church see Catholic
  Church

Second World War
  anti-fascist tradition, and 103–4
  civil war after 1945 103–4
  corruption during 123
  distorted memory of end of 13
  Italian losses 102–3
  Italy's surrender (1943) 5–6
  Mussolini's 'mistake' 102–6
  popular memory of 125–6
  propaganda 151–2
  resistance to German occupation
    102–3
  unpreparedness for 124–5
security see control
self-image 16–17
social insurance see welfare system
socialism, socialist movement
  blacklisting against 39
  complicity with fascist regime 49–50